Juliana,

May the Light be with you always!

Sofia Seitchik

# The Light of Deaf Women

Stories from Visionaries, Artists, Founders and Entrepreneurs

## Sofia Seitchik

# ACKNOWLEDGEMENTS

**Creator**
Sofia Seitchik, Global Deaf Women

**Book Coordinator & Assistant Editor**
Irina Normatov, The Wealth of Joy

**Content Editor**
Lauren Putz, Fireproof Editing

**Creative Editor**
Rachel McConnell

**Photographer**
Clare Cassidy, clare cassidy photography

**Image Descriptions**
Keri Brooks, TRUE-BIZ ASL

**Digital Retouching Artist**
Andrew Ian Rubin, digitAIRmedia

**Cover Design**
Michelle Lapides, dozanü innovations

The information contained herein was obtained by interviews done in 2016-2017 with subjects who were chosen based on criteria set in 2016-2017. Neither Publisher and Author shall be responsible for any errors, omissions, or claims for damages, arising out of use, inability to use, with regards to the accuracy or sufficiency of the information contained in this publication.

E-mail: info@globaldeafwomen.com
Website: www.globaldeafwomen.com

Printed in the United States of America

First Printing, 2018

ISBN: 9781543919721

You will see the acronym ASL used in several stories in this book. ASL stands for American Sign Language, the primary method of communication for many Deaf women featured here.

Image descriptions for DeafBlind and Low Vision are provided on page 190.

# Introduction

The vivid tapestry of today's world is woven with millions of Deaf women, remarkable individuals who are a silent staple of our everyday life. In every community and every industry, there are brilliant, tenacious, and empowered Deaf women working and thriving. But there are not many places where we can share our stories: our journeys, struggles, pains, frustrations--and ultimately, successes. The purpose of this book, which has been a dream of mine for many years, is to bring Light and inspiration to the world, and especially to the Deaf community.

Your Light is your inner drive; the way you communicate with your soul. Light is what makes you want to lead a meaningful life and make a difference in the world. Be we Deaf, Deaf-Blind, Deaf-Disabled, or hard of hearing, each one of us possesses a unique gift that contributes to the world and reminds ourselves how amazing we are. By finding and shining your inner Light, you elevate your being and others around you. It is my hope that you will feel a connection to some of the women featured here.

My own inner Light came from years of fighting for opportunities. At three years old, I was sent to school in Russia, away from my family in Uzbekistan. My mother and father, who always believed in me, knew that if I had stayed in my home country, I would not be afforded the opportunities that came from my education in St. Petersburg. They gave me the gift of wisdom, the drive to persevere, and instilled a high sense of self-worth. If not for my parents and my sisters Ada, Nellie, and Irina, I would not be who I am today. I created this book also as a thank-you to them, for allowing me to discover my Light.

I would like to give a very special thanks to my husband, David Seitchik. He is my backbone in running my business, Global Deaf Women, and in running our family. David is always there for me and pushes me to believe that I can continually go farther in life. Our children, Eitan and Samuel, are my biggest inspiration. Thank you to my in-laws, Murray and Hope, for their neverending support and encouragement. I am very fortunate to work with my sister, Irina Normatov, who has been with me as my right-hand person through every high and every low. I would like to express my deepest gratitude for her fierce dedication in every retreat and project, especially for this book, and her great contributions to the success of Global Deaf Women.

Special thanks also go to my dedicated editorial team who helped make this book possible: Clare Cassidy, our photographer; Irina Normatov, project coordinator; Rachel McConnell, creative editor; Lauren Putz, content editor; Michelle Lapides and Katherine Lees of dozanü innovations for marketing and designing the cover; and finally, thank you to every woman who shared her story here. Thank you for putting your hearts into this project.

Much Love,
Sofia Seitchik

# Contents

# Iris Aranda
## Irisne Fine Arts

When she was little, Iris Aranda used to play with papers in her father's office. "My dad thought I was wild with ADHD," she says. "But my mom saw that even though I was so young, I had artistic skills, so she decided I should take art classes." From the time she was eight to the time she turned twelve, she took art classes to hone her skills. Born in Panama, her parents sent her to school in Argentina, where she first learned how to communicate. Later on she went back to Panama to learn how to speak orally.

She was discovered by the hearing art community through the classes she took and her work ended up being published in a book. When she was 22, her paintings were displayed in an exhibition and shared around the community. There were judges who saw her artwork and wanted her to show her paintings in art galleries, which excited her parents in particular. She quickly created 30 more paintings and was able to sell 15 of them, and from there she decided to set up her business, which she calls Irisne Fine Arts. Her repertoire includes various types of artwork, such as sculpture and woodworking.

Before she was exposed to the Deaf community, she explains that the hearing art community offered her a different perspective on selling her work as genuine artwork. She then met Chuck Baird, who praised the art Iris was making and encouraged her to embrace her identity in her art. Of course, having Chuck Baird's stamp of approval let Iris know she was on the right track. "He helped me understand how Deaf art can be used as education, and my Deaf identity in the Deaf art community," she says. Iris wishes she had understood her identity prior to setting up her business, because it helped her know who she is and be proud of the woman she's become.

She has dreams of setting up her own studio in New York City, and currently contacts galleries in order to sell her art and increase sales for her own business. "I stress sometimes about providing the best work possible," she says, particularly due to unique challenges as an immigrant and Deaf woman. One challenge she faces coming from a Spanish-speaking country is being able to communicate with gallery owners in English. "I use Video Relay Services where the interpreters can translate from Spanish to English," she says. Regardless of the barriers she faces, Light for Iris is about finding the right time to express her creativity, which is why she honors her nocturnal nature by creating her artwork at night.

**"My best advice for young women in the age of rising technology is to take art classes and discover their art."**

# Irma Azrelyant

## *Deaf and Hard of Hearing Interpreting Services, Inc.*

For Irma Azrelyant, going to work is like going to a birthday party every single day. Every morning she's excited to get up and start working at her agency, Deaf and Hard of Hearing Interpreting Services. Irma is grateful to be able to serve a community that she cares so deeply about, and also feels that she can provide exceptional interpreting services since she is Deaf herself. "I personally understand what it's like when you get interpreting services that exceed your expectations," she says. She also meditates and practices daily affirmations and sees gratitude as the Light inside her.

Irma's journey begins in Kiev, Ukraine. Irma fell in love with interpreting as early as five years old. "I'm hard of hearing, but I come from a Deaf family, so I would interpret for some family members like my grandmother," she says. She immigrated to America to begin a new life with her husband and two children. In college, she worked as an intern for an interpreting agency, and once she graduated, she started up her own business with a partner.

There were many challenges and lessons she learned throughout her journey of running an interpreting agency. She cites her life coach as someone who has been her biggest mentor and ally. "During my worst times and after making the wrong decisions for my business, I crashed," she says. "I knew I needed to ask for help. That was the first step." She worked hard at reassessing herself and her business and rebuilding the trust she lost from the Deaf community. During this process, she grew her Light. "After working with my life coach for several months, I began to grow into a new Irma," she says. She recognized her strengths and weaknesses and was able to find the will to go on. Her best advice to Deaf young girls wanting to pursue their dream? "Never give up, do your best. Always do your best."

Today, Irma continues to grow her Light by maintaining a balance between her two loves--her work and her family. She now has five beautiful grandchildren. She continues to provide interpreting services within the NYC area, recently winning contract bids for large health systems and nonprofit organizations. She also maintains a free newsletter she established, *Deaf NYC News*, that compiles and shares popular upcoming events. "It is an amazing thing to be able to give back to a community of which I am a part," says Irma. "It has taught me much about humility and gratitude. This is my home."

**"Live every moment. Laugh every day. Love beyond words."**

# Ally Balsley & Brittany Noschese

## Hand Waves Birth Services

Birth is an incredibly sacred experience, and every birth has its own story. Families who are expecting or who have given birth benefit from as much support as they can receive, and that is where Brittany Noschese and Ally Balsley come in. As birth and postpartum doulas, they educate, honor, support, and nurture families in their journey prenatally, during birth, and postpartum, through Hand Waves Birth Services.

Naturally, their journeys into the birthing world began with the births of their own children. As mothers, both women found that each birth experience was astonishingly different, and there was in fact an abundance of resources available for expecting and new families. The challenge? They weren't accessible. Being instinctive caretakers and educators--Brittany wanted to be a veterinarian growing up, and Ally wanted to be a teacher-- the women partnered up to provide families with resources, support, and education that are accessible in sign language.

The birthing world is full of beautiful people with big hearts, and their organizations are often small and not-for-profit. Brittany and Ally appreciate the opportunity to connect with other birth workers in their area and it is quite difficult to get ASL interpreters provided at these events. The issues are always funding, lack of information, small organization size, and so on. This just fuels their passion--to be able to make their services accessible to the ASL community.

An essential skill for Brittany and Ally to run a business successfully is to be mindful. Being aware of one's responsibilities and paying attention to the moment with calmness and clarity helps one be more focused and open to challenges. This helps create valuable change and leads to many other important skills such as collaboration, having a positive attitude, being less stressed, and overall better health.

As a doula, no two days are alike. Every day is unique, unpredictable, and an enthralling adventure. No matter how the day goes, they go home with an even bigger heart after seeing that their services have made a difference.

**"Light means every birth story is beautiful."**

# Michelle Angela Banks
## Mianba Productions

When Michelle Banks was a young girl, she knew she wanted to be an actor. She fell in love with acting when she first saw a strong Black female character in *Sounder* played by Cicely Tyson. Since then, she has been portraying strong characters onstage and onscreen. She loves to explore different avenues of communicating with people through expression of the arts, and considers it an absolutely essential skill to running a business. "Focusing on communication is key to learning how to approach people with respect," she says.

Michelle took acting courses at Gallaudet University and subsequently with the Conservatory of Theatre Arts at the prestigious Purchase College in New York. Michelle then founded Onyx Theatre Company in New York City, the first deaf theatre company for actors of color in the United States. "I believe that my theatre work has helped change many lives by breaking down the barrier in the show industry, opening doors for Deaf actors of color in entertainment, and giving them the opportunity to showcase their talents," says Michelle. "I believe that I'm the creative force of my life by sharing my talents with people and telling stories about Deaf African-Americans." Her work has recently earned her the 2017 Laurent Clerc Award for her contributions to the Deaf community.

One such contribution, creating roles for Deaf women of color, is paramount because she recognizes she has to be aggressive about approaching people for opportunities and creating her own work to show the world who Deaf women of color are. "Being the Light means finding out who you are. You need to know your destiny and your purpose in life," she says. "Follow that Light and believe in yourself. Don't let negative energy get to you."

Striving to be her absolute best, Michelle uses a variety of tactics to keep moving forward. "Prayer, meditation, and believing in myself," she says, to name a few. "Whatever challenges you face in life, you got to get in touch with your soul or talk to someone who has experienced life challenges." Sometimes as an actress it's difficult for her to accept rejection or competition, but she reminds herself to be persistent and follow through with her dreams. "I know I'll reach my goals regardless," she says.

**"Be the pioneer of your own dreams by seeing the impossible to make a significant breakthrough."**

# CyEra Bibbs-Taylor
## Sparkle Divas Makeup Artistry

Growing up, CyEra Bibbs-Taylor had always wanted to be a fashion designer. She loved the whole fashion industry and was fascinated by all its different elements, including--and especially--makeup. But life happens, as it does, and she found herself working for a company called Chimes until she got pregnant with her daughter and went on maternity leave. After her daughter was born, she found out she was involuntarily terminated from her job.

With a newborn at home and no job, she pondered revisiting her dream of working in the fashion industry. CyEra then went straight to an aesthetics and skincare program to learn everything she could in order to become a makeup artist. From there she began her business, Sparkle Divas Makeup Artistry, and has worked with clients for a wide variety of occasions. Her services include theatrical makeup, editorial makeup, bridal makeup, T-shirt design, and anything she can do to bring out the beauty of sparkle in every person she meets.

She says the best piece of advice she ever received came when she was just starting out and trying to set up her business. The tip? Keep failing.

CyEra admits that she did not promote herself as much as she should have. "The failure is that I did not speak positively about my work and my experience," CyEra shares. "I have learned to shift from a negative space into a positive space, and the more I promote myself in a positive way, the more clients will come!"

CyEra is an avid believer in the notion that as long as we consistently keep trying for our goals, our failures will lead the way to success. She is also a strong advocate for community and strives to inspire positivity and growth with every client interaction in addition to making them look and feel beautiful. Currently, she is working on launching a cosmetic line, Sparkles4Divas, and would be the first deaf woman to own a cosmetic line.

Although she sometimes must sacrifice family time and personal purchases for her business, CyEra knows how important it is to invest in your work and the community you are serving. She cares deeply about her clients and their needs and wants to show the world exactly who she is and what she is capable of--and in doing that, her best self is brought out for the world to see.

**"When it gets hard, give yourself a day to regroup so you can get right back on it, full of power!"**

# Keri Brooks
## *TRUE-BIZ ASL*

Keri Brooks considers herself to be a Jill of all trades, working as a Certified Deaf Interpreter, ASL specialist, ASL professor, and workshop presenter. In addition, she is the CEO of an online ASL/Interpreter education business she founded with her partner J. Sam Harris, TRUE-BIZ ASL, which also provides interpreting services. The pride and joy of their business is the Deaf Interpreter Training Online program, the first and only program that provides comprehensive training online to Deaf Interpreters from all over North America. As the demand for online interpreter training increased, they were filled with delight when the program quickly became a huge success, and they are proud to share their expertise and tools.

Coming from a long line of business owners on her father's side, Keri isn't surprised she ended up carrying on the tradition. However, a surprising collision of events back in 2014 is what really got the ball rolling. She unexpectedly decided to leave her marriage at the same time her ASL teaching career maxed out, leading her to move to Florida to begin teaching interpreter education at a university. However, midway through the semester, she was suddenly let go.

"As devastated as I was," she says, "I had no idea what the future had in store for me. As a result I decided to take a break from the job search until I could figure out what was next." She continued to teach at another college while she took a little bit of time for some introspection. Ultimately, it took her life partner, Sam, now also her business partner, to ignite the spark. "We work together really well and that has been essential when we experience different challenges," Keri said. "Owning a business together, it can be stressful for couples to focus only on each other. We enjoy going on international trips to reconnect with one another."

Keri considers being Deaf a true gift. She is blessed with unique communication skills to connect with people from all walks of life, whether they are hard of hearing, DeafBlind, speaking a foreign language or otherwise. Top-notch communication accessibility is Keri's incentive for TRUE-BIZ ASL's interpreting services, in order for more connections to form among people. Keri believes in sharing our knowledge and our experiences with one another to encourage others to shine their own Light and pass it on.

**"Without Light, we cannot know ourselves, our true potential, or our place here on Earth and within the Universe."**

PROD. Nº ShatteredMind
DIRECTOR Jade
CAMERA Al Rivera

| SCENE | TAKE | ROLL |
|-------|------|------|
| 41A | 12 | 7 |

# Ann Marie "Jade" Bryan

## *Jade Films and Entertainment*

Frustrated by the lack of opportunities for Deaf Talent of Color in Hollywood, Jade Bryan formed her own business to give herself and others jobs. "I've been following my passion since film school in 1991," she says. "The industry is still not ready to hire a Deaf full-time writer or director in Hollywood Studios." Through her company, she produces a variety of documentaries, video campaigns, commercials, educational videos, films, community events, and multimedia projects. The company also works with other organizations and businesses to form alliances that encourage cultural arts and awareness in the community.

As a senior at New York University in 1991, she was hired as a production assistant in a paid internship to work on a movie called Boomerang. Jade did everything from office work to on-set production work. Through the experience of working on a Hollywood studio production, she knew this was her calling--to tell stories. Later, she found a mentor. "This mentor advised me to take up entrepreneurial workshops, attend small business seminars, consult with lawyers, and get as much information as possible before setting up my business," she says. "Of course, I went through several trials and tribulations, but I learned a lot through that."

She believes strongly in bettering herself in order to raise the bar. "It's up to them to catch up; I ain't waiting for them," she says. As the first Black Deaf filmmaker, she is a trailblazer and pioneer to many people in the industry and Deaf community. "One of my greatest achievements so far was winning 16 awards for a film I created called The Shattered Mind," says Jade. She submitted her film to over 200 film festivals globally and 44 festivals selected her film to show. "Whenever I get a rejection, I submit another. Getting a rejection doesn't necessarily mean I should stop doing it or that my work isn't good," she explains. "There are many reasons for the rejections. People need to learn to incorporate the word rejection as a motivator, not as a failure."

A staunch career woman, she has no desire to settle down or have children. "I am an artist and a creative force," she says. "So much of my time and energy is invested in my creative work." She encourages young Deaf girls to try everything they can at first. "Experiment; pay attention to that fire in your soul," she offers. "Participate in STEM programs and find a mentor to guide you in pursuing your passion." She utilizes the law of attraction and garners as much positive energy as she can in order to stay focused and accomplish her goals.

**"Quit? What's that? Never heard of it."**

# Patty Carter
## PattyCakes Mobile

Growing up living next to her grandparents, Patty Carter used to sit in the kitchen and watch as her grandmother baked cakes, pies, and desserts for the holidays. She was her grandma's taste tester, always trying out the different batters and flavors but shying away from actually baking. It wasn't until her grandma passed away that Patty began thinking about how to pursue something in the field of baking, and in fact credits a dream she had as the inspiration to dive into her business.

"I was following these cupcakes along a path, and there, sitting at the end and smiling, was my grandmother," she describes. "It was like she was telling me to go ahead and start this business." Patty had obtained a degree in Digital Imaging and Publishing, but was having difficulty finding a job in that field. She ended up working at National Deaf Academy and Maryland School for the Deaf until she decided to become a stay-at-home mom. The only problem? She was bored out of her mind. So Patty started baking desserts, sharing the extras with her friends and family, and they encouraged her to sell them. This encouragement, coupled with the dream of her grandmother's blessing, propelled her to leap forward and open her business.

With PattyCakes Mobile, she creates all her cupcakes from scratch and either delivers them throughout Frederick, Maryland, or brings them to festivals, where she sells them from her booth. "I work every weekend from spring to fall and at farmer's markets on the weekdays," she says. "My goal is to get a cupcake food truck or even set up my own shop." Patty notes the exhausting demands of constantly traveling to work in high-noise, fast-paced environments, but she says support from her friends and family is what has gotten her through.

"There are moments when I just want to stop, and they'll remind me how much I love seeing customers' faces when they first take a bite of my cupcakes," says Patty. It's a grueling business to work alone, but she powers through every experience she has--good or bad. "You'll learn many things throughout your journey," she counsels, "But once you know what your skills are, work for your dream." She struggles with not being home very often and feeling like she sometimes she just doesn't know what she's doing. Without a business partner, it's difficult to want to persevere with all the ups and downs, but Patty says the Deaf community has been her reason to keep going. "If it wasn't for them, I probably wouldn't see this through," she says. "They have given me so much support."

**"Light is seeing my customers take a bite of a cupcake and smile--that brightens my day."**

# Clare Cassidy
## clare cassidy photography

Clare Cassidy is mainly known as a photographer, but you can see that she is more than just that. Her photos chase moments, capture them, and give us the gift of stunning stills. She loves light itself and especially how the term *photographer* means "writer of light." For her, there is no profession as perfect. Clare is living the dream, fully immersed in a career brimming with her passion.

As a little girl, she used to sit in a corner and read pages and pages of *National Geographic*. She spent hours poring over each photo and daydreaming that she'd one day be a photographer for them. Fortunately for her, her parents were very supportive, back in the days when one had to pay for each print. Their unconditional support cemented her lifelong dream: to become a traveling photographer.

Clare's passion was touch-and-go until she became ill and had to take disability leave. Her doctor encouraged her to partake in a hobby that would keep her happy and distracted. Thus, clare cassidy photography was born. She quit her day job to focus on her business, and admits that while she is concerned about financial stability, she could not allow her spirit to die because she needed "stability."

With her three sons, Clare is embarking on an exciting journey where they will travel across North America living in their RV full-time. Her travels will culminate in a book titled *finding meraki*, which is a Greek word that means putting your passion into a piece of artwork. It is a dream come true for Clare, and she looks forward to sharing it with her boys. Clare credits her husband and twin sister for being her pillars of support, keeping her balanced and inspired.

She cannot imagine not being a photographer. For Clare, Light is passion, the air she breathes, and the very being of her soul. She is also a very outspoken activist for women's rights and Deaf children's rights to language acquisition. The best advice she can give to any woman who wants to start a business is to never submit to inferiority imposed by a male-driven society and to always persist.

**"The art of writing with Light holds the greatest appeal in humanity; it informs, it shares, it evokes emotion, and it creates a legacy that lives on."**

# Maleni Chaitoo
## Producer and Actor

After graduating from Gallaudet University with a Bachelor's degree in Business Administration, Maleni Chaitoo tried her hand at quite a few non-business jobs before landing a role as a producer for the comedy web series, *Don't Shoot the Messenger*. She'd worked in museums, in education, in film, and in coffeeshops until her dogged spirit earned her a role with the YouTube series.

Maleni has a knack for seeing problems as opportunities for her to create something extraordinary. When there appeared to be no chance that the digital marketing and advertising company she'd been interning for was going to hire her permanently, she left. She used the time afterward to critically study a range of different fields, and this blessed her with a great network for project opportunities.

"I have plenty of fire in my belly," Maleni asserts. "Which means I have to be ready to fight with my energy, beliefs, and determination." As a Deaf Indian woman from New York City and a daughter of immigrants from Trinidad and Tobago, she educates people to be conscious and sensitive about Deaf people of color--including herself--and their needs. "It requires a lot of work and patience to do," says Maleni. "But sharing your Light is an example of participating and contributing in an honorable way."

She considers one of her greatest achievements to be receiving a filmmaker's grant from New York Women in Film & Television in order to complete the first season of her web series. Maleni has also advocated for people with disabilities and given speeches representing non-governmental organizations. She's also appeared in quite a few different works as an actress, most notably in an episode of the Netflix original, *Master of None*. Her favorite part of her work is collaborating with teams and sharing magical visions together.

**"Do not be afraid to ask for help. That does not mean you are less smart or less capable of reaching your dream, that means you'll have support to lift you higher beyond your expectations."**

24

# Patricia Ward Costello
## *Herbal Soothing*

For 14 years, Patricia Ward Costello worked as a teacher at Marie Philip School for the Deaf. In fact, it was Marie Philip herself who taught Patricia to embrace life as a Deaf woman with a strong Deaf identity. "This motivated me to become a compassionate educator, supporting every individual to lead a full, productive life regardless of any barriers or obstacles they faced," says Patricia. But she wasn't always so confident in her identity as a Deaf woman. She originally wanted to become a dental hygienist, but at that time, the profession was unheard of for a Deaf person. Patricia switched her major to Art History/Museum Studies before realizing she truly wanted to teach Deaf children.

One day during her first year at Gallaudet University, she was on the bus with a friend when the friend began signing and Patricia told her not to sign in front of hearing people. "I was embarrassed using ASL in public, only using it within my Deaf community. I did not want hearing people to notice that I was different," she says, speaking of her adolescence. Taken aback, the friend bluntly told her, "Let people know that we are proud to be Deaf and show them we sign and we can educate them." That experience made her realize she should not hide her identity. "I thanked her for that moment of awakening, one that had a huge impact on my life," she says.

In her adolescence, Patricia also suffered from severe eczema. "I would scratch my entire body until my skin was raw and bled," Patricia recalls. "Nothing helped, so I decided to read books on various treatments." She realized essential oils were effective in treating her eczema due to their antifungal, antiviral, and antibacterial properties. The healing power of these natural plant oils led her down the entrepreneurial path as a desire to help others improve their lives. Patricia's grandmother grew up on a farm and cherished herbal plants; this became the seed of Patricia's business, Herbal Soothing.

When Patricia was first starting out, creating her own innovative products didn't happen overnight. She had to study and experiment with different herbal products, but without interpreters at workshops, she found herself developing her assertion to work with instructors one-on-one. "I sell homemade, chemical-free natural products, including essential oils," Patricia says. "My products help soothe the soul with natural aromatherapy. The teacher in me allows me to share the benefits of my products in ASL with the Deaf Community."

Being around nature provides her with time to meditate, so that she may receive spiritual messages from the Universe for continuous support. Patricia encourages other women to find the Light within: "Don't give up until you find what sparks the Light in you, then your journey is right."

**"Let every moment of every day be a blessing and let me spread that joy to all. Let all my beliefs be positive."**

# Julie Dalbom

## Reproductive Rights Activist

In this day and age in America, it is often already difficult enough for people to get access to reproductive health care. For the Deaf community, it can sometimes be next to impossible. That's where Julie Dalbom comes in, an HIV/AIDS volunteer advocate who now considers herself a reproductive rights activist. After losing friends to HIV/AIDS, Julie was incentivized to become a volunteer advocate in Colorado. Soon she was being contacted by Deaf people with questions about reproductive health care and how they could get access to information and resources. When she moved to Maryland, she was contacted by many Deaf students at Gallaudet University who had no idea where to find resources or what to do regarding STIs, birth control, abortion services, and general reproductive health. "Eye-to-eye with these terrified, confused students who had no idea what to do or what had happened, I noticed a pattern of hearing people making decisions for Deaf people," she says.

According to Julie, there appears to be a widespread belief among hearing people that Deaf people do not have sex. This dangerous misconception, coupled with a language barrier, leads to deaf people being systematically underserved. They do not receive equal access to education like they deserve, specifically in sexual and reproductive health; they may not know how to protect themselves and access resources. Julie found striking parallels between anti-choicers and the hearing world in terms of their desire to control others' bodies. "As if our bodies are for others to enforce decisions upon; as if they don't belong to us," she remarks. "You have the right to bodily autonomy--the right to sign or speak for yourself, and the right to make the best decision for your body and future."

She now takes to the streets in an orange vest marked "Clinic Escort" in the ASL alphabet in order to assist patients that come to a clinic for the procedure, protecting them from protesters outside the clinic. She is also working with nonprofit organizations that fund reproductive justice projects nationwide in order to increase awareness about the lack of information on Deaf people and reproductive health. Her goal is to empower the Deaf community to ensure they have full bodily autonomy, especially concerning reproductive health and their rights.

**"The best advice I've ever been given? Gather information and understand, but leave your judgment out. You are not in anyone else's shoes."**

# Julia "Jules" Dameron

## *Film Director and Actor*

"Do it. If it's what you really want to do, then do everything in your power to improve your skills to become the best at it. You'll be unstoppable." This sage advice comes from Julia "Jules" Dameron, who spent her directing career proving herself to be the equivalent of any professional hearing male director out there. All her life she'd been aware of her identity as a Deaf woman, so she sought--and fought--to be on top of her game in the film directing world.

Led by her ambitious personality, she applied for a random film directing gig she found online. She got the job and suddenly found herself in charge of a cast and crew of 40 people. "I had a lot to prove because my producer was still skeptical I could direct hearing actors well without hearing them talk," she says. "I fought my hardest to stay ahead of everyone." When it was finally finished, it was submitted to a film festival. Jules had low expectations, but much to her surprise, she ended up winning Best Director--a moment she now remembers as the "biggest validation" of her life. When they handed Jules the award, they actually had no idea she was Deaf.

She has since directed a TV series in Norway called *Møkkakaffe*, created countless ASL music videos, and founded Deaf Women in Film. Jules also coined the term #Deaftalent, which propelled a movement calling for executives to start hiring Deaf actors for Deaf roles instead of giving them to hearing actors. It is one of her many visions to see Deaf talent perform to the point of ultimate success in the entertainment industry.

So when Jules was approached by DPAN TV in the hopes of setting up a sign language channel, she was thrilled. She is currently working with them to construct a creative space for Deaf individuals. "A creative environment must always be cultivated and encouraged," she says. Jules knows sharing your Light means being willing to give out everything that you've worked your hardest for to others that may need it too.

**"You are 100% in control of your thoughts, reactions, feelings, and your body. Not your parents, family, friends, or even society is in charge of you. Once you fully realize that, you're one of the most powerful beings on this planet."**

# Julia Cameron Damon

## *Magical Mystical Massage Tour*

When Julia Cameron Damon was 23 years old, a friend gifted her with a certificate for a massage. Having been raised in an extremely conservative family, Julia felt anxious about the idea but decided to go only because she didn't want to offend her generous friend. Looking back, she describes it as a pivotal experience that put everything in perspective. Shaking on the table and hardly able to breathe, Julia remembers the therapist as an "angel of patience" whose nurturing manner helped her let down her guard. "I felt the air slowly release from my lungs and my chest unclench. I knew one thing: I had to learn how to do what this lovely woman was doing to me," Julia says. She set out to study at the very same school this therapist had, but it took the school 17 years of requests to provide interpreters before she went.

The most ridiculous piece of advice anyone ever gave Julia came from the president of that world-renowned massage therapy school. "It's not your dream," she told her. "Find another one." Julia says that bad advice was perfect for her at the time--because she knew that president was wrong. "It taught me to trust what I knew in my heart to be true," she says. "I knew I had been called to do this. Gut instinct is crucial to a happy life and meaningful work."

After studying there, she worked all over the U.S. and Canada in spas until she decided to start up her own office, Julia Cameron's Magical Mystical Massage Tour. In addition to massages, Julia is an artist who does portraiture, murals, painting, and costumes. The art she is most known for is her Body Paint Photo Shoots, which require a full day and can be done in almost any location. "I wanted to be more generous with my time," says Julia. "Both art and massage are all about connecting with someone on a deeper level, slowing down enough to really register another human and what they want to share."

One challenge she has faced is not allowing well-meaning people to haggle down her prices. "I'm not trying to be the cheapest artist or massage therapist; I'm striving to be the best I can by always learning and evolving," says Julia. "This absolutely warrants a living wage." For her, massage is about listening to the individual, bearing witness to their stories, struggles, and triumphs. She likes to create a safe and loving environment so people feel free to work through whatever comes up. "We all just want to feel heard," says Julia.

**"We are all worthy of--and need--self-care. Each person deserves to recharge and needs 'me time' to be their best selves."**

# Brenna DeBartolo

## Forest Souls

Brenna DeBartolo grew up listening to her inner soul as an artist and photographer. At one point, she wanted to experience the corporate world, despite many people silently warning her about how toxic that environment can be. After working with one company for nearly three years, her energy was completely drained and her creativity was constantly blocked. "I just thought, this is not who I am, and I need my soul to grow by doing what I love," she says. Brenna feels we as humans are disconnected from our planet. "Nature didn't build cubicles, we did," she says. "I decided to make a change by asking myself how I could use my skills to contribute to the environmental community." She resigned from the corporate job, and Forest Souls was born.

Brenna travels deep into forests throughout America and she designs unique products that capture the natural essence of her atmosphere. With Forest Souls, her socially-conscious modern clothing line, all 60-plus design ideas have sprouted from forests. Brenna's mission is to make each Forest Souls customer feel inspired, refreshed, and connected with nature while wearing her clothing line. Together, Forest Souls works with American Forests to protect and restore forest ecosystems across the U.S. and throughout the world--to date, Forest Souls has planted over 900 trees, a few for each item that Forest Souls customers purchase.

Brenna recognizes that running her own business certainly comes with its own challenges. In particular, the communication mishaps that arise from being a Deaf businesswoman in a largely hearing industry sometimes slow her down. However, Brenna tells herself not to allow fear to get inside her head. "Fear should be afraid of me," she smiles. Her determined mindset has taken her far in order to get to where she is now.

Brenna's philosophy is that we are put on this earth to study living things and that nature is the key to unlocking our capabilities as we learn how to connect with the world around us. The meaning of Light to Brenna and to Forest Souls is people being true to themselves by doing as her motto says: "Create. Grow. Balance." She hopes to inspire the community to connect with nature and shine their own Light in order to be at peace with themselves and the world around them.

**"Listen and stay connected to your inner soul all the time for your queendom to exist, and never stop maintaining it."**

# Kelly Doucet-Simpson

## Kelly Simpson Photography and Oil Painting

The best Christmas present Kelly Simpson ever received was waking up to a pony in her basement. Kelly loved horses and began drawing pictures of ponies when she was a toddler. Her parents encouraged the development of her art skills by signing her up for adult painting classes. "I would take classes without an interpreter," Kelly recalled. "Every time I visited an art gallery, it made me realize I wanted to create art."

Kelly majored in Photography and Museum Studies and took a job as a museum curatorial technician. After 19 years of grinding away, she had a burst of inspiration: she would return to her love of photography and painting animals. Growing up with a deep, untouchable love for animals, Kelly believes each and every pet has a soul that is interconnected to the person fortunate enough to care for it. She strives to capture each pet's everyday look through a contemporary style, using bright background colors that draw attention to the pet's personality. Before she begins painting, she interviews the client to find out the pet's personality, and even meets the pet if possible.

Today, Kelly's lifelike paintings and stunning photographs are found in many homes across the nation. Her work has also been on display in numerous shows, galleries, and exhibitions in Frederick, Maryland; Toronto, Canada; and Washington, D.C. since 2013. She is deeply grateful for the many family members and friends who always encouraged her-especially her dear husband, who believes in her unconditionally. Without the support of the people around her, Kelly isn't sure she would have started selling her art at all. "I didn't see myself selling until someone was persistent about buying it," she says. "I wasn't sure if I could succeed in business as an artist." After attending a retreat for Deaf women called Power of Me and receiving advice for moving forward with her business, Kelly gave it a try and set up a booth to sell her artwork with Global Deaf Women. To her surprise, people fell in love with her art, sparking a burst of confidence inside her that gave her momentum to keep creating.

After the initial insecurity, Kelly's spirit thrived once she began sharing more and more of her art. She credits social media as an indispensable tool, receiving most of her custom orders after updating her pages with progress pictures for her paintings. She also hosts "painting parties" where she teaches eager attendees to paint their interpretation of some work of art. As Kelly paints, she constantly communicates with the developing portrait before her, and works to illustrate the animal's spirit in its expressive eyes. This is Kelly's way of appreciating animals for their unconditional love, their comforting presence, and their special purpose. Kelly's advice to others who want to pursue their passion is simple: don't be afraid to be amazing. Be comfortable with your gift.

**"Don't wake up with problems in your mind. Get up feeling good. Stay focused on being positive."**

"Do joyful things,
and joy will be circulated like fresh air."

Monique Holt

# Crystal Eusebio

## Assistant Director of Student Activities, Boston University

If you go to the Student Activities office at Boston University, the first person you will meet is Crystal Eusebio, a proud first-generation Deaf Filipina-American woman. Standing at merely five feet tall, her job makes her larger than life. She provides event management and resources to over 500 campus organizations, handles campus-wide programming, and oversees campus safety. Crystal thrives on seeing the impact she has on students who are meeting a Deaf woman of color in a leadership role when they first walk into the office.

Connecting personally with her students and seeing them reach their full potential is what she loves most about her job. She relishes the opportunity to share stories and languages with people who are part of all different kinds of communities. She urges young Deaf girls to have faith in people--that they will see them for their true potential, not their Deafness. Crystal was fortunate after her graduation to land a full-time marketing job in California, but found that what she had always envisioned as her dream career was actually a disappointing letdown. When she worked at home without a support system, it isolated her. In fact, she went against her instinct when she accepted that job--and learned never to ignore her instinct again.

Fueled by her frustration, Crystal made a bold move 3,000 miles away to the East Coast to find herself and to find her new dream. It took three years of lacking guidance and feeling utterly lost, but ultimately this pushed her to pursue her Master's in College Student Development and Counseling. She wanted young adults to know that the struggle of feeling lost is part and parcel of finding the light at the end of the tunnel--just like how she landed the perfect job at Boston University.

She draws upon her own experiences and feelings when she's guiding students. Crystal considers the cross-country move to be one of her greatest achievements, creating a new home with a new social network and a new dream job. Her journey to where she was today all fell into place serendipitously. It made her capable of sharing her Light with other people in the same spot in their lives. Her bottom line? Trust your instincts, always.

**"The Light to me means the Universe, my intuition, and my guiding force."**

# Jasmine Garcia Freeland

## All That Jazz

Jasmine Garcia Freeland believes in going all-out in the pursuit of your dreams. "You have one life--just one!" She exclaims. "Why aren't you running like you're on fire toward your wildest dream?"

She began running toward her dream of becoming a jewelry designer after 15 years of teaching had finally burnt her out. This came about after giving birth to her child and going through postpartum depression, and at first she had no idea what she wanted to do anymore. One day, she decided to have a little "me time" and went shopping, where she came across a book called *Hero* by Rhonda Byrne. "I finished that book in two days. Bam!" she says. "I told my husband it was time for me to do something I really love to do."

Jasmine has always known she wanted to do something with art, so she began developing her ideas and designs and within a year, she had launched her business--All That Jazz. At first she was determined to do everything herself, but quickly realized the key was support from her family as she navigated all the bumps along the way. "I had my share of low moments when I felt like my business was slow-growing," she says.

But in the first two years of running her business, she learned so much that has propelled her to success. "Once customers feel like they can connect and talk to me, they're much more comfortable," she explains. "It helps them know I'm not all about selling things but rather someone with listening eyes and an open heart." Because of this, she also was able to gain a better perspective on what her customers are looking for and what they like so she could tailor her website to their needs.

"I tend to process ideas at 100 miles an hour," she laughs. "At first I worked 24/7 nonstop, but it got to the point where I actually crashed and got really sick for two weeks--and I still couldn't stop working." When her son finally came to her and told her he missed her, she broke down in tears. From that point on, she made sure that her schedule always included family time and that she had a healthy balance between work and home.

For her, the patience required and the time sacrificed is worth it to do what she really loves. She recognizes that she didn't feel like her for many years, and she has grown into a better person by running a business she believes in.

**"My vision is to empower women to feel beautiful about themselves."**

# Karen Carlson Freitas

## Treasures From Trees

At 14 years old, when most children spend their summers anxiously awaiting high school, Karen Freitas was working a full-time summer job as a horticulturist. Growing up working in the garden with her parents had sparked her love for forestry, landscapes, and wildlife conservation. She continued working during the summers in every forestry job she could find--planting trees, trimming trees, maintaining state parks and landscapes, and even woodworking in her parents' gift shop, Legend of Bigfoot. Karen comes from a family with a passionate love of all things nature, which is how she and her parents eventually ended up going into business together.

Upon entering high school, Karen took many wood shop classes and enjoyed woodworking so much she decided to turn it into her career alongside forest management. She now runs a small business called Treasures From Trees, where she manufactures wood products and finished furniture to be sold to local gift shops. Her goal is to someday sell her unique wood furniture at the Log and Timber Home Shows.

She developed several forest management plans on her properties over the many years. Her dad started the California Forest Improvement Program, and in training with him, she eventually developed a plan for conservation of the forests on her private land with the Natural Resource Conservation Services. Her goal is to expand forest practices to include things such as herbicide spraying, road access, wildlife management, and the like. She is also one of the first Deaf women in America to work on many projects in the Environmental Quality Incentives Program under the United States Department of Agriculture. Karen currently owns 160 acres of forest in California.

"I love working in the mountains," says Karen. "It gives me breath, peace, and beauty." Forestry is her favorite kind of work, which she fondly remembers learning from her father as she was growing up. Two years after she became business partners with her parents, they both passed away unexpectedly in the same year. "It hit me really hard. I cherish everything my parents gave me," she says. "I know my parents are looking down at me, smiling and proud." She honors their legacy in the form of the business they started together, Treasures From Trees.

**"I get my shining Light from the Deaf community, because they are so important in my life--I want to do something to be able to give back to them."**

# Alice Ann "Alli" Friends

## Friends Interpreting Services

When Alice Ann "Alli" Friends decided to become her own boss, her unbounding enthusiasm was halted by two pregnancies that blessed her with two sets of twins. She was forced to put her business on hold so she could focus on finding a job to support her family. But once she reignited her vision, she worked incessantly to grow her business into the full-fledged interpreting agency it is today. Growing up, Alli was given little opportunity to succeed. "I came a long way from where I was," she shares. "I was treated very differently, and I was very, very behind in my education and social skills."

Alli recalls how important it was for her to try a number of odd jobs once she graduated from college. She worked at Maryland School for the Deaf, Kinko's, Disney, and Things Remembered, but it was her job with Sign Language Associates that inspired her to create her own business. Her passion for her work at the interpreting agency propelled her to take a leap so she could be her own boss. Having the experience of working for various companies helped her narrow down exactly what she wanted so that she could pursue it.

Indeed, Alli has spent the last several years channeling her efforts into Friends Interpreting Services, while raising four kids with her husband, without whom she says she couldn't have done it. Her most persistent thought over the last six years has been *Should I give up?* But she always remembers the support of the people around her, including one mentor who likened owning a business to playing a game of chess: "You move and you never know the outcome. You just have to keep trying."

Today, she has excelled to the point where she is a GSA Schedule holder with the federal government and a Small Business Association (SBA) 8(a) certified firm. The long hours and difficult years of feeding the fire with drive, persistence, and dedication have proven to be worth it for Alli. She loves working from home, and recognizes that never giving up is a feat in itself. She keeps shining because her mission is to show the world that Deaf women can do anything.

**"You never know if you will get there until you try and see the Light! Big opportunities will stand above the rest."**

# Dr. Suzette Garay

## *Baby Signs 4 U*

Dr. Suzette Garay has faced adversity from the beginning. As a little girl at a very young age, she yearned to be a psychologist, but was told by her social worker that she couldn't achieve that dream because she was Mexican, came from a dysfunctional family, grew up in multiple foster homes, and later on that she was too Deaf. That didn't stop her. Today, she is an educational psychologist and a psychology professor, teaching a variety of classes at a local college.

She knew she was different--but chose not to let it define her. In fact, that very choice is the foundation of her private practice working with many families and adults toward accessibility and self-advocacy. Naturally, that led to teaching families of hearing babies sign language and other special needs children who many believed would not be successful.

There were many moments of self-doubt for Dr. Garay, though, such as when she was ten years old and about to move on to another foster home. She found a quiet place at school to hide and cry until the janitor found her. He wrote a beautiful message on a piece of paper and handed it to her. It said, "There is nothing anyone can say or do to change the way you feel about yourself; only you can do that."

She still carries that piece of paper with her today. She also carries the memory of her last moment with her biological mother on her deathbed, where Dr. Garay stayed with her until she passed. "I never really knew my mother, but I leaned over and told her, 'I forgive you, and I'm okay. You can go now,'" she says. "It was then that I realized if I could forgive my mother, I could forgive the rest of the world for all their wrongdoings...then I could be okay."

As an accomplished motivational speaker, Dr. Garay has the honor of being the first Deaf Latinx woman to receive a PhD in special education. She is a lifelong student, always thirsting for knowledge and giving back to the next generation of young Deaf children and women who need to know it's possible to achieve their dreams.

**"Light is seeing the lighted up smiles and sparks in the eyes of the children when they realize that someone finally understands them."**

It isn't *what* we say or think that defines us, but what we DO.

-Jane Austen

# Arlene Garcia
## Veditz

For Arlene Garcia, going from a K-12 high school principal to a startup entrepreneur took a leap of faith, but her family is no stranger to leaps of faith. Her Deaf parents moved to New York from Puerto Rico, where they raised their daughters in the Bronx. "They both came from Spanish-speaking families, so you can imagine all the communication barriers," says Arlene. She is particularly sensitive to language barriers as she has observed a huge gap in academic resources and communication access that impacts many Deaf children in K-12 schools.

Because of her experience with various roles in the field of education, when Arlene decided to resign as the K-12 principal for Colorado School for the Deaf and Blind, she was determined that she could no longer ignore the issue plaguing Deaf education. Arlene had such a deep desire to improve the lives of Deaf children that taking the chance was worth it--so she created Veditz, the first mobile, on-demand, live interactive video chat tutoring, education, and practice platform for K-12 Deaf students. Veditz covers a variety of topics, including instruction and tutoring in ASL, English, Mathematics, People's Character Traits, and Vocational/Career Skills.

"Being the visionary person for Veditz has been a gift to me," Arlene says. "I love and believe in the product that we've developed specifically for improving education in college subjects and beyond for over 70 million Deaf people." It is her passionate hope that Veditz will provide an opportunity to break the communication barriers that are often present between hearing parents and their deaf child. As there is no comprehensive program available for parents to learn how to communicate with their deaf child, Arlene is striving for Veditz to be the first program to provide hearing parents and deaf children with an interactive learning product with self-paced lessons and activities.

As a single mom of four children, Arlene manages to juggle the workload of a new business while parenting. Sometimes it's easy to become discouraged at the continual waves of challenges, but Arlene believes in perseverance. What helps her most is being organized and being able to predict and plan outcomes.

Arlene deeply values learning and she encourages others to learn as much as they can. It is her belief that once we understand more and we move ourselves forward, only then are we able to advance the world around us. "We know there is a Light within every person as strong as a thousand suns, and that Light always comes from each person's inner self," she says. For Arlene, there is always an opportunity to use that Light to connect, educate, and empower the Deaf community nationally and globally, which is what she aims to do with Veditz.

**"Share your stories. Inspire others. Empower their light."**

# Haydee Garcia

## Go Haydee Tours

Haydee García is one of the most dedicated, energetic, and enthusiastic advocates of the Deaf in Cuba, having been born and raised there until her emigration to America, where she currently resides in Chicago. "Nothing is accessible in Cuba for Deaf people," she says. Growing up, she attended a deaf school but otherwise often relied on her parents for access and understanding. Upon graduating high school and attending a technical institute, she even earned a degree in computer programming without any interpreters or Deaf-accessible services.

Even with her degree, she had difficulty finding employment in Cuba due to widespread misconceptions about Deaf people there. But once she finally found work at the National Association of Cuban Deaf (ANSOC), she quickly found ways to foster success for the Deaf community. While in that two years of working with ANSOC, and with the City of Havana Association of the Deaf, Haydee actively worked with her team to create the first-ever dictionary of Cuban Sign Language. She was also instrumental in initiating changes in the school system to mandate the usage of Cuban Sign Language in teaching Deaf children and developing a national curriculum to train the network of interpreters throughout Cuba.

After being blacklisted in Cuba and unable to work, she immigrated to America and made her longtime dream come true when she enrolled herself in Gallaudet University. During her time there, a busy Haydee served on the Student Senate and also as President of the English Language Institute for two years, eventually becoming a United States citizen in 2006. Her activism and accomplishments at Gallaudet earned her the honor of being the 2007 graduating class speaker. As she met more and more Deaf friends there, they expressed their interest in visiting Cuba, which became the catalyst for starting her business, Go Haydee Tours.

Go Haydee Tours aims to provide accessibility for Deaf tourists using ASL. Organizing Deaf-accessible travel tours in Cuba from America presented a slew of problems for Haydee, the most hindering of which was governmental. "Socialism is different than capitalism," she explains. "I can only use the resources that are available in Cuba for American tourists, and restrictions make it difficult--sometimes tourists get stuck trying to go to Cuba, or banks are unwilling to work with Americans." Still, Haydee never lets the struggles stop her. Haydee's company currently offers 7-day and 12-day tour packages in Cuba and is working on expanding to Mexico, Ecuador, and Argentina. She is determined to see Deaf locals employed and living comfortably in Cuba. "I never forget about my home, my country, and journey," says Haydee. "I always come back and remember."

**"Go and start a business now, do not waste your time. That 'later' will never happen. You'll learn so much more now. It is never too late!"**

# Claudia Lorraine Gordon

## *Lawyer and Disability Advocate*

When she was an eight-year-old child living in rural Jamaica, Claudia Gordon suddenly lost her ability to hear. She was taken out of school and kept at home, only leaving with her family on trips down long, winding, bumpy roads to distant towns. "Healers would perform rituals in attempts to cure me of my deafness; soothsayers would read my palms to predict when I'd become hearing again," she remembers. "Friends disappeared and the usual cheerful hellos became forced smiles, curious stares, and even outright ridicule." Claudia felt hopeless, confused, and struggled to retain her dignity and her sense of purpose.

Because of her own experience with various forms of discrimination and oppression, she decided around her high school sophomore year that she no longer wanted to be a victim. "Instead, I wanted to contribute to a better society where there is more understanding and acceptance of people with disabilities, and where the same opportunities are provided for all," she says. Instead of perpetuating a victim mentality, she decided to use her experiences as stepping stones. She found her own voice and she was determined to use it in amplifying the voices of the unheard--so she made it known that she was going to be a lawyer and vehicle for change.

Claudia chose to attend the undergraduate program at Howard University, a hearing historically Black college, and she credits this as one of the best decisions she's made on her journey. Despite feeling alone and isolated, she found a silver lining in sacrificing peer connection by being able to focus entirely on her goals. "Growing up, I witnessed my mother's hard work and sacrifices as she struggled to raise my two siblings and me," she says. "As a domestic servant with only an eighth grade education, she literally scrubbed her way to America one garment at a time." When her mother arrived in the South Bronx, she continued working to ensure she would be reunited with her children, who eventually immigrated to America as well.

Since graduating with her law degree, Claudia has held several significant positions. She spent more than seven years with the Obama Administration serving as Chief of Staff of the U.S. Department of Labor's Office of Federal Contract Compliance Programs and as the White House's Disability Liaison in their office of Public Engagement. She is now Sprint Accessibility's Senior Manager for Government and Compliance. "Choose to be defined not by your limits but by your potential," she encourages. "We're all born with our own set of strengths and weaknesses--regardless of our individual circumstances, it is up to us to nurture and develop our potentials." She wishes she had known that it's okay to own her identity and power and urges young Deaf girls to not let voices of doubt dictate their worth or their capacity.

**"Sharing my Light means rising above the narrow confines of my own individualistic concerns to embrace the broader concerns of all humanity."**

# Melissa "echo" Greenlee

## deaffriendly

Melissa "echo" Greenlee's vision is simple: she wants to create a Deaf-friendly world. After graduating college, she went from job to job. "In every job, I would eventually reach a point where others felt I was not capable to move up any further because I was Deaf," she says. Year after year, as others continued to dictate their own ideas of her ability to achieve success, her belief in herself only grew stronger. "In my mind, the only way out of others' limitations on me was leaving the workforce and starting my own business," she says. "When I did, I was finally free of their limits. Now, the possibilities are endless."

The aim of deaffriendly is to create a platform that allows Deaf people to rate and review businesses based on how Deaf-friendly they are. "Who better to educate the hearing world about our unique needs than Deaf people?" echo surmises. Growing up in a hearing-dominated world, she is well-practiced in self-advocacy. "It's an unnecessary hardship, and people's ignorance about Deaf people is the foundation of our hardship," she says. "So after years of challenging experiences as a Deaf consumer, I thought: how can I make this easier?"

Recognizing that many hearing people have never met a Deaf or hard of hearing person in their lives, she likes to think that most people are receptive to learning with a little bit of guidance. That's why she made a decision to dedicate her life to helping people understand the Deaf experience to promote openness and acceptance. "The world taught me to be hearing-friendly," she says. "Now I teach the world to be Deaf-friendly." In addition to running deaffriendly, she also sits on two nonprofit boards, the Disability Rights Advocates in Berkeley, California and the Hearing, Speech & Deaf Center in Seattle, Washington.

"I'm not afraid to put in the work, challenge myself, be vulnerable, learn from my mistakes, and work on my shortcomings," says echo. "On occasion, I'm overcoming fear, self-doubt, self-criticism...I'm not perfect, but I attempt to do my best. That will have to be enough." She is an entrepreneur, wife, mother, friend, and more; so many roles to cover, it can be tough to balance her time as running a business requires a wide range of skill sets. "Some skills come naturally to me, others take much effort to execute, and some I will never master," she says. "But at the end of the day, I can always rely on my intuition."

**"Be authentic and vulnerable. It makes you relatable."**

# Smitha Hanumantha

## TheZenobias

A Virginian by way of the India that bore her, and quite literally, a billion others, Smitha Hanumantha graduated from Rochester Institute of Technology with a bachelor's degree in graphic design and Gallaudet University with a master's degree in administration and supervision. She has since worked odd jobs such as on a boat, as an Apple Guru, and as Gallaudet Administration Assistant Extraordinaire, as she describes it. "I'm never satisfied with simply sitting still--hello, have you met me?" she quips. She utilized every tough barrier in every life experience of hers to arrive to where she is today. "The best part of this whole thing? I'm still not done," she says with a smile.

As an Indian-American woman hailing from the other side of the world but growing up in Virginia, she was surrounded by people who were nothing like her. Slowly but surely, she learned to build her fort of resiliency while developing an artistic mindset to help her navigate different obstacles--and along the way, she fell in love with fashion. Through her work, absolutely loves being able to generate unique ideas and considers it extremely important to understand and honor imagery from the different cultural lenses by which her life is intricately designed. "I take time to travel to other countries and learn about different cultures," she says, "so that I may continue to be inspired to inspire."

It was a mentor who instilled in her the confidence and belief in her own ability to leverage her skills in marketing, graphic design, and project management. "That's when I started to realize I should offer my services through my own business," she says. And boom--TheZenobias. With her new business as a designer and fashion stylist, Smitha is able to represent her own creativity for others, providing creative personalized digital and graphic design services as well as bringing an affordable fashion consultancy. Most clients come to her with a specific cultural vision, and it is up to her to create something in harmony with their values. "How can I Zenobias you?" is her tagline.

She admits that at first, she used her lack of business acumen as a reason to put off her business. "But I quickly learned and realized I need to listen to my intuition and follow through," she says. Thinking about the future, gauging the success of her projects, and finding new customers and clients are all challenges that weigh heavily on her, but she keeps in mind the importance of work and life balance and daily self-care. "Society may dictate certain norms, but fashion is about breaking the rules--it is okay to be a maverick," says Smitha. "It's about telling your story, sharing your fashion, and allowing your own identity to shine."

**"Seek to build a network of people who can complement you by bringing their strengths against your own weaknesses."**

# Laural Hartman

## *Dirtybeardpress*

Laural Hartman has always been fascinated with the beauty of letterpress printing, the overlapping waves of colors evoking depth and richness. Letterpress printing is a technique originally used in Germany to print text, images, and patterns onto paper. "As a Deaf person with only four of my five senses, it was only natural to have an urge to touch," she says of the printing blocks. After finishing her Bachelor's degree in Illustration, she knew she wanted to run a creative business of her own, but instead found herself stuck in a job she didn't like-- exhausted and burned out.

In the midst of planning her wedding around the same time, Laural was searching for letterpress wedding invitations but couldn't find a design she liked at an affordable price. "So I thought, *'Why not just make my own?'*" Shortly after, her and her husband relocated to California for his career. "I was broke, jobless, and depressed," she remembers. "But it was an opportunity for me to start from the bottom. I used my last paycheck to purchase a printing press, and it was the best career decision I ever made." Laural owns three printing presses weighing in at 6,500 pounds total, all bigger than the majority of her possessions.

At first, she didn't realize how much effort it would take to run her business alone. From designing the products and maintaining the website to taking orders and shipping them out in time, it was too much to handle without another person on her team. She recalls sacrificing hours upon hours of her time to work on projects in order to get her business going. "Sometimes you just have to do it," she says. "There's no such thing as being in the wrong place or doing it at the wrong time."

Laural and her husband now reside in Rochester, where they run their printing business, Dirtybeardpress. She loves the therapeutic nature of working with tactile products and sharing them with her clients, Deaf and hearing. For Laural, the Light within her grows brighter the more she shares it with others. We crave, thrive, and live on Light.

**"You have to find what sets you apart from others. Anyone can develop a skill, but no two people think exactly alike."**

# Lisa Hermatz, Lauren Maucere, & Kavita Pipalia
## KODAWest

As Deaf mothers of hearing children, Lisa Hermatz and Lauren Maucere began seeking out resources for their families only to be met by exasperation due to the lack of services for KODAs (Kids of Deaf Adults) on the west coast. In the United States, around 94% of Deaf parents have hearing children; however, programs for this demographic were few and far between. They got together to discuss the importance of parents being well-informed and well-equipped to empower their KODAs with tools to help them embrace their multifaceted identities, and found themselves inspired to provide those tools themselves. As they were working to establish a solution, they were introduced to Kavita Pipalia, another Deaf mom of hearing children who was equally frustrated with the lack of support for KODAs in the area. Together, they became the impetus for KODAWest--the first nonprofit organization that provides year-round programs such as workshops, mentorship, and annual camps for KODAs.

In addition to working full-time and raising children, Lisa, Lauren, and Kavita dedicated much of their time to their vision, and the three women were the driving force behind KODAWest for the first 12 years. They have witnessed countless KODAs blossom into proud individuals who no longer struggle with their identities. These children gained a better sense of self, a whole new community, and a network of support, and numerous parents have expressed profound gratitude for the constructive transformations they have seen in their kids. Knowing the impact they have has been one of the most rewarding "paychecks" for these moms. One teen camper told them that camp was only the place she could be herself and feel free.

Lisa, Lauren, and Kavita express their deep gratitude for the support of their community: families, friends, and KODAs. "Without them and their belief in us, KODAWest would not have been as successful as it is today," they say. It indeed takes a village of dedicated volunteers who share the same passion as these three mothers to achieve the mission of enhancing of the lives of KODAs out there. Their constant and uniform message to all the Deaf parents of KODAs: "Be sure to let your children know they are nothing short of awesome, and that there are many others just like them." At the end of the day, their goal is to help all KODAs embrace and cultivate the wonders of their unique identities.

**"When we spread our love and light, we immediately ease others' stresses or sadnesses. When you have given the person the push they needed, they will, in turn, push another person in need!"**

# Peggy O'Gorman Hlibok
## Educator

As a teacher, learning has been a huge part of Peggy O'Gorman Hlibok's life. She studied at Gallaudet University, Queens College, and Union College, with a Master's degree from New York University. In turn, she has since worked as an educator for more than 20 years, in K-12 and college classrooms. She also gives presentations regarding the Deaf and Hard of Hearing community, and has an impressive list of accomplishments as an activist.

Peggy was a full-time stay-at-home mother of four children until her last child, Nancy, enrolled school full time. She decided to become a part time New York University student and part time NYU researcher, where she fell in love with being an educator. During her NYU work, she interviewed deaf adults in several cities across the United States, collecting ideas and suggestions for the closed captioning projects. In addition to teaching, she also served on the New York State Commissioner's Advisory Panel (CAP) for Children with Disabilities for fifteen years, becoming one of the strongest proponents of a bill that passed in the State of New York. It required them to use the term "deaf and hard-of-hearing," rather than more incendiary terms such as "hearing-impaired" or "deaf-mute".

Her four Deaf children and their spouses, along with ten CODA's and one deaf grandchild, went on to become incredibly successful adults. Raising their children with unconditional love and instilling the value of family life, Peggy and her husband, Albert, a construction cost consultant, would start supper each evening as a family by singing "Go Lucky and Be Happy." After supper, the family debated various topics of deaf/hearing life, politics, social issues, and leadership. This all happened over the very same kitchen table Peggy uses today--a wedding gift from her in-laws 60 years ago.

With an innate understanding of the importance of being a team player, Peggy led by example, being the president and secretary of the Empire State Association of the Deaf, New York Governor Mario Cuomo's Delegate to the White House for the Handicapped, a co-founder of Mental Health Association of the Deaf in New York, and founder of the first deaf elder camp in the US, located at the Camp Mark Seven site. She also worked toward the implementation of the ASL curriculum for the State of New York. She spent seven long years fighting for the recognition of ASL as a second language for public schools. Her experiences in helping the Deaf community have helped her understand people better and grow as a person. "We can all learn from each other," she says. "We are to educate others with what we have been educated."

**"To me, the Light of Deaf women means that Deaf women are ready to face and solve problems in life that help make them smarter."**

# Elise Nye Holliday
## Santa Fe Weaving Gallery

Elise Nye Holliday's turning point was a culmination of years of sacrifices and working the corporate ladder for what she thought were all the right things: a beautiful home, a stable career, and the coveted material trappings. The time to dive into a new calling came when she realized she had given up her own creative passions along the way. "It became a driving need to pursue those," she says. "I had always made so many thoughtfully-analyzed decisions, but I had to push past my fears and forget the risk in taking a fall."

She wishes she had known before she started her business not to hold so many of her fears and doubts inside. "Inside my own head, they festered and grew unbridled; whereas, if I had exposed more of them, they would have been examined in the light of day," she says. Today, she is running a high-end boutique called the Santa Fe Weaving Gallery, representing over 50 small-studio clothing designers and surface fiber artists from around the world.

Elise acknowledges the path getting there was not an easy one, however. "The path you embark on often involves shedding layers of darkness, untangling rootballs of emotions and thoughts, building strength and clarity, dismantling inherited beliefs and social structures," she says. "It is hard--as Life often is--but it is such a worthy path to pursue."

These days, she is seeking a reasonable balance between her personal responsibilities and her responsibilities to those in her circle. "My journey was prompted by a deep longing for a more meaningful life," says Elise. She has designed a life around her business and family like she wanted, and in doing so has achieved flexibility and the fulfillment of being independent. "Now, the biggest sacrifice is time with my children," she says. "Though I may have less time with them, the time I do have with them is quality, and my children gain a fulfilled mother."

**"Sharing my Light is sharing my unique enthusiasms and challenges to show that everyone is different, and what turns us on is unique--yet, we all share a common humanity."**

# Tawny Holmes

## *Education Advocacy Lawyer*

When Tawny Holmes was younger, she jumped from one career dream to another depending on what inspired her at the time: swim instructor, librarian, and forensic scientist. It was not until high school that she determined she wanted to become a lawyer focusing on education advocacy. This desire stemmed from seeing her language-deprived peers struggle in school growing up and from learning about civil rights movements, such as Deaf President Now. There was no easily accessible role model, since only a handful out of 300 Deaf lawyers in the U.S. focus on education advocacy. This did not stop Tawny from pursuing her dream.

After Tawny successfully completed law school, she applied for a public interest fellowship, building on her years of volunteering for the National Association of the Deaf (NAD). This fellowship enabled her to create her dream job, traveling all over the country to provide training and collect information about the state of education in each community. Today, Tawny works for the NAD as their education policy counsel, advocating for language access for all Deaf children. The community has always looked to the NAD to provide services and resources when it comes to Deaf education, but due to limited funding and support, the NAD was unable to commit much staff time or resources--until they won two fellowship opportunities, one of which was the Equal Justice Works fellowship that Tawny received. In doing so, Tawny made her own dream come true.

In advocating for deaf children's language access, Tawny is able to see the light at the end of the tunnel because when people are out there, doing something, things will change. Tawny believes that in doing so, faith is needed, along with the ability to connect with people.

Looking back on her career and life, Tawny credits her deep passion for her work for maintaining her drive on a daily basis. However, Tawny reminds women with passion that we have to be mindful that we cannot be everything for everyone, because if we forget ourselves, we cannot maintain our energy for our dreams. And if there's one thing that Tawny wishes she knew at the beginning at her journey, it's that behind every situation, every person has a story, and that story has a lot to do with how that person interacts with the world.

**"Life is about making the best out of it. Advocacy is about making it better for others."**

# Monique Holt

## Actor and Director of Artistic Sign Language

Monique Holt was a freshman in high school rehearsing for a production of *Fiddler on the Roof* when she was told by her ASL coach that nobody would want to buy a ticket to see her perform because nobody would be able to understand her signing. Flash forward many years later, she is now working as an actor, director, and all-around artist. She has even spent the better half of those years working as an ASL coach, Director of Artistic Sign Language, and translator for many productions. Of her freshman performance in *Fiddler* she says, "I just cried and cleaned up my signing. I didn't know sign language would be a huge part of my career."

Growing up in a dysfunctional family, she developed a unique empathy that she believes made her the strong person she is today. Monique places great emphasis on creating her own happiness. "Happiness is about finding your center and owning your identities, gaining a better understanding of yourself," she says. Though she describes it as a complicated, lonely journey, she says she's realized that many people simply need to hear that they are not alone. "So I share my stories with them, and I believe it helps people find hope," says Monique. "Life's scars aren't ugly--they strengthen our character, and through telling our stories, we find better ways to understand life."

Her biggest challenge is time management, since working as a freelancer presents a conundrum: she creates her own schedule, but she is often working under clients' schedules as she is not always her own boss. Monique relies on her unofficial team of support around her to help her through crunch time, such as friends who support her spiritually and mentors who generously give their time and wisdom.

As direction, she offers this to young Deaf girls on the cusp of opportunity: start your own tribe. "Each person in your life serves a different purpose, whether to inspire you, to push you, to offer a shoulder to cry on--it's important to have more than one ally," says Monique. "They'll open up the world to you through their own networks, which will not be the same as yours." This, she explains, is how you expand your opportunities--because you can't do it alone.

**"Light is a necessity in life, illuminating the mystery and enlightening our purpose."**

# Sabrina Hottle-Valencia

## *Simple & Fit*

During an internship working as a personal trainer her senior year, Sabrina Valencia jumped into the world of fitness and never looked back. She has long since been passionate about living a healthy lifestyle centered around an attitude of positivity, but when she saw the lack of accessible information in the Deaf community, she knew she wanted to play a part in providing that information. "I wanted others to be able to experience the life I'm so passionate about," she says.

In pursuing this life, she gave up the security of a stable future. With her bachelor's degree in Communication Studies and her master's degree in Deaf Education, her background offers little in the way of her new business, Simple & Fit. Sometimes the instability of running her own business gets to her: Sabrina questions whether she's doing the right thing, knowing she has little security in her future. But when that fear creeps in, she merely reminds herself she is doing something she is passionate about. "That's worth the sacrifice," she says.

She now works as a fitness and lifestyle coach to help provide support to the Deaf community in fitness and health, creating programs and services tailored specifically for them to make it possible. Sabrina has also competed in 10 of the National Physique Committee's Bodybuilder's bikini division competitions and won first place four times. "I love inspiring others, encouraging them by being an example myself--showing them that a healthy lifestyle is possible," she says. Sabrina considers herself a passionate innovator and presses young Deaf girls to work hard for their dreams. "Nothing is easily given," says the fitness coach. "Know that it may be a long journey, but it'll be well worth it."

After seven years in the business world, she's learned a few tricks for success in business. Having a strong foundation by doing things like establishing a business plan, sharpening your technological skills, and building your relationship with your community will go a long way. "Everything is a learning experience for me, and I'll never want to stop growing and learning how to be better," says Sabrina.

**"Light, to me, is a way for all of us to travel through life as best as we can and continue to embrace who we are."**

# Vicki Hurwitz

## Pioneer and Deaf Women Herstorian

Vicki Hurwitz always dreamed of becoming a professional dancer; but when she was a child, there were no Deaf dancers to look up to. It wasn't until years later that she would learn of a Deaf dancer on "The Lawrence Welk Show." This is why Vicki is so passionate about sharing stories of Deaf women--she wishes she knew back then that there were Deaf women out there who succeeded at their goals regardless of the barriers against them.

Discouraging remarks from peers and the lack of Deaf role models as a kid in the 1940s led to poor self-esteem, which Vicki has worked to overcome by building a strong system of support around her. Through her rich and varied experiences, she discovered abilities and confidence in herself she never knew she possessed. Vicki credits her husband of 52 years, Alan--former president of both NTID and Gallaudet University--and her friends for their belief in her. They pushed her to pursue jobs for which she did not think she was qualified.

Vicki considers service a rewarding part of her life, and she has been an eager volunteer since she was a teenage "candy striper" in a children's hospital in Missouri. She completed her bachelor's in social work at age 39 and master's in career and human resource development at age 49, both degrees at RIT. Since then, Vicki has worked as a social worker, peer sexuality educator, Coordinator of Student Development, Director of Outreach, and co-founded Deaf Women in Rochester in 1981 and Advocacy Services for Deaf Victims in 1998--both of which are still going strong. Today, she continues to research and present on Deaf Women's HERstory, her passion for more than 30 years.

Her life's journey brought her with Alan to House One on the Gallaudet University campus, where Vicki served as First Lady for six years. Upon discovering the elaborate hidden history of House One, she helped get the beautiful lithophanes restored and opened up the residence to visitors for tours and events, sharing a vital part of Gallaudet's history. She was curator, narrator, and producer of the documentary on House One's cherished history. As the honorary Chair of Friends of the Gallaudet University Museum, she was involved with the opening of its Deaf HERstory exhibition. The fight against her own lack of self-confidence has paid off, and she encourages others to reach for their goals with confidence. For Vicki, Light is taking pride in who she is.

**"Let's enhance the path for a brighter, barrier-free future for young Deaf women so they can leap to new heights!"**

# Dr. E. Lynn Jacobowitz

## ASL STAR

Dr. E. Lynn Jacobowitz is a comedian full of wit and full of love for ASL. Having adopted two Deaf daughters from Eastern Europe, ensuring access to ASL resources is near and dear to her heart. The decision to adopt the girls--one from Bulgaria, and the other from Russia--came after a trip to Egypt where Dr. Jacobowitz witnessed homeless children living on the streets, who did not realize they had so much potential. The trip, which was a five-week Deaf teacher education program training for the State of Egypt, as a part of the U.S. AID Project, cemented her commitment to signed language access.

Preserving the history of Deaf art and ASL is a strong passion for Dr. Jacobowitz, who started her journey into business as the President of the American Sign Language Teachers Association. After ASL Rose, the only resource for first-language ASL users at the time, lost support and had to fold, she was inspired to establish ASL STAR (Services, Training, Arts, and Resources) to serve the Deaf community. When she learned that there was no official assemblage of ASL or Deaf memorabilia, Dr. Jacobowitz took it upon herself to categorize, collect, and compile buttons, cartoons, videos, T-shirts, and any other products created by the Deaf community. With ASL STAR, she hopes to someday publish a history of Deaf paraphernalia.

ASL STAR is a multifaceted company, but its primary role is to provide and refer ASL "athletes," or experts, for ASL and ASL-English bilingual teacher education programs, ASL-Deaf comedy shows, and ASL-Deaf community advocacy and building services. Dr. Jacobowitz also works to promote ASL legislation all over the United States, most notably setting up the National ASL Legislation from 1995 to 2001 and increasing the number of states that recognize ASL as a language from 22 to 38 states.

Dr. Jacobowitz wishes she had studied business in college, noting the mistakes and financial downfalls she experienced while she was building her business. She recommends starting with the Small Business Administration in order to get a business loan, something she wishes she had done instead of getting personal loans. For young Deaf girls, she advises dreaming big, but starting small in order to achieve.

**"The inner light is my rhythm of my divinity, peace, and Universe."**

"We can't keep the light for ourselves without passing it on to others. The light shines even brighter when there's a WE, rather than I. Inspiration inspires!"

Melinni Taylor

# Rochella Jones

## 5 Wellness

Rochella Jones grew up with an idyllic childhood, memory conjuring up images of bare feet on an organic farm. "We didn't use medicine," she explains, her family instead opting for superfoods, herbs, and natural remedies. She left her parents' treasured home in Minnesota to pursue a Bachelor's degree from Gallaudet University, but soon felt called to return to her family's farm--Living Food Farm, where she worked in customer support and research. After some time, however, she was struck by the vision of running a business of her own. Leaving the farm was a painful process, but she knows her rich experience at the farm led to the bite of inspiration for her own dream.

At around the same time that she left, her sister Ronda was looking for information regarding holistic health and wellness online, but found that almost all the videos available are spoken in English without any captions. Frustrated by the lack of access to information related to holistic health, she would ask Rochella to clarify the confusing information on the internet, and Rochella would give her advice. "Ronda suggested I set up my own business and sell supplements through a website, providing the information in ASL so that Deaf customers could understand," says Rochella, who initially resisted the idea. She was doubtful that people would trust her without any credibility in her background, but couldn't shake the idea--and the more that her sister encouraged her, the more she gravitated toward the concept.

As a resolution, Rochella decided to take courses to get her certification in Holistic Nutrition Consulting. She then took it upon herself to create 5 Wellness and open up access to health information on her website by providing videos in ASL and one-on-one consultations in order to empower Deaf individuals in their own well-being. To date, she has created over 100 videos in ASL, amounting to thousands of hours of work. In addition, she owns 20 hens at her coop and sells organic eggs. She also honors her mother's recipe by making homemade strawberry leather from real berries and raw honey, one of her most popular and fast-selling products.

Whenever she's worried about failure or making mistakes, she remembers this advice--that the process of building a business takes time, and customers are the primary concern. To this day, she has led her business with that philosophy, keeping integrity at the core of her company. "You have to keep going and trust your instincts even when you feel like nobody is supporting you," she advises. "No matter if you feel you may fail, you have to try." Rochella loves motivating others to pursue their own passions in addition to educating them about health so that they may improve their lifestyles.

**"Light is like an ember in a soul that cannot be dissolved with water."**

# Leah Katz-Hernandez

## Public Speaker, Advocate, and Communications Consultant

As the first Deaf Receptionist of the United States in the Obama administration, Leah Katz-Hernandez is well-versed in the costs of ambition: fatigue, burnouts, late nights, early mornings, lots of associates but few friends. Growing up an avid reader, she dreamed of someday becoming a writer, bringing happiness to other children through her stories. Still today she is deeply passionate about improving others' lives, and works tirelessly to show the world everything Deaf people are capable of. She initially started out working for President Obama's re-election campaign in 2012 before being appointed as Michelle Obama's press assistant and research associate. "After a year on the job, the challenges began to grate at me," she admits. "I was making mistakes because I was so worn down by the grueling physical, mental, and emotional challenges."

As the demands and responsibilities of her job increased, the tiny mistakes she would make were often public, recognized, and attributable to her, exacerbating her stress and weighing her down. One day, a beleaguered Leah made a mistake that was the final straw for herself personally. "I completely broke down," says Leah. "Everyone likes to fantasize that they're stronger than the challenges facing them, but the reality is, we're all human and they will affect you." After calming herself down, she moved past that day and stuck it out. One thing she knew would never be an issue: she refused to quit and she refused to leave.

A few months later, she was asked if she'd be interested in interviewing for a job in the West Wing. When she became the Receptionist, interviewers began calling her a role model. "Your dream is worth more than just you," Leah tells people, young Deaf women especially. She explains that as Deaf individuals trying to accomplish our goals, we must overcome more challenges than our hearing counterparts--but when we do, we inspire and impact communities all over the world. "Your success brings hope to generations both young and old," she says.

Her desire to better the lives of others still runs strong, and she now works as a public speaker, advocate for the Deaf, and communications consultant. In reaching for her dreams, Leah is adamant about never giving up. "Never consider leaving something because it's 'too hard,'" she says. "Yes, things are hard. But you can do it. End of story." Leah, with all her ambition, has learned what really matters. "We often talk about ambition and reaching high--but ultimately, what's more important is grit."

**"Light is the embodiment of hope. In dark times we look for the light, and when we find it, it fills up our space and helps us find our way toward our goals."**

# Mara Ladines

## By Mara

Mara Ladines took her dream of being a fashion designer all the way to California State University, Northridge to study fashion design. One day, she was asked to imagine setting up a business. "They asked what our logos would look like, and I knew I wanted to create one that showed exactly who I am--a Deaf Filipina woman," says Mara. Wanting something universal but still representative of her Deaf identity, she chose to use the I Love You sign as her logo. Instead of going to her formal graduation ceremony, Mara had her own celebration at her home in California with a fashion show from her collection. She gifted her family members with items emblazoned with her logo as a token of appreciation. People were interested in the products she had made, but she wasn't interested in selling them. Still aiming to become a fashion designer, she soon ran into challenges due to the competitive nature of the fashion industry.

After months of job hunting, Mara was discouraged. The state of the economy at the time meant heavy competition, and she struggled to get interpreters for her interviews. With encouragement from her family, however, she decided to put her logo on T-shirts and begin selling them. She was only intending to test it out, but it was successful--and she shifted her passion to starting her own business, By Mara.

"I thought my logo represented me, but really, it was about everyone," she says. "It's about people being part of the Deaf and signing community, and it's about who we are." She was simultaneously running her business and working in retail when her husband at the time got laid off. Mara was tirelessly supporting them with two incomes. "I forgot all about our marriage," says Mara. After they separated, she struggled for several years to cope until the separation was finalized. "I was falling apart; I almost gave up everything," she admits. "I was ready to throw away my business."

Fortunately, Mara had a very kind friend who helped run her business while she took care of herself. "That's when I realized my family and friends are my biggest supporters," she says. "If it wasn't for them, my business would have fallen apart." She escaped to New York City where she revived her business in Brooklyn. Mara says her business is her life and that it drives her to work passionately every day. Her shop, By Mara, is located in the trendy neighborhood of Dumbo in Brooklyn.

**"You owe it to yourself to be who you are."**

# Michelle Lapides & Katherine Lees
## dozanü innovations

The Universe often throws mysterious twists our way, and nobody knows this better than Michelle Lapides and Katherine Lees. The two were laid off from their jobs within one month of each other--a life-changing event that challenged them and their confidence. In the end, that low point became a turning point that prompted the duo to take a long look at one another, their desires, their passions, and their purposes in life. For them, it felt like the beginning of "Life" as it was meant to be, taking the layoffs as a blessing in disguise to break free from traditional routines and expectations.

With this fresh perspective, dozanü innovations was launched. The company offers support to entrepreneurs in their journeys by providing an alternative perspective based on inclusion-focused marketing and business design strategies that jumpstart ventures, ideally propelling businesses to the next level. "Ultimately, we want to bring together all creative and talented people to formulate a powerful force of innovation, making the world of business a circle of talents and resources," they say.

The two are unique, young Deaf women co-running a business in addition to being life partners who are crazy about each other. "The business development industry is very male-dominated, so we're excited to bring in a modern feminine perspective," says Katherine. "The first step is to embrace that dozanü innovations is a company owned by two wonderful eclectic and talented Deaf ladies," chimes in Michelle.

For these women, their business is all about finding the inner passion in people and their businesses, ultimately for the greater good. "When you ask me about sharing and shining my Light, it is about being raw and authentic," says Katherine. "And sharing my Light means sharing my authentic inner self so that all those who also have passionate inner Light may find the confidence to accomplish something bigger as a community."

"Life may throw you something that is better than your five-year plan. Take the plunge!" Michelle says. These ladies are all about taking risks, doing what your heart desires, working hard, and reaping the rewards life gives you, even small wins. The two ladies embrace celebrating each and every victory. Michelle and Katherine both know they've gained much more than they've sacrificed in their adventure.

**"Experience as much as you can--experience everything, everybody, everywhere you go! But make wise choices; the impact will be everlasting."**

# Rosemary Latin

## *Rosemary's Fabulous Cakes*

At her low points, Rosemary Latin isn't wishing for her days to be better. She moves to create herself to be better. "I have a gift with the power of creating positive change," she says. "I keep my eyes and heart open." She was initially working a humdrum job as an optician making glasses, but found no challenge in it. "That was when I started making cakes for my sons' birthdays, and a friend encouraged me to start up my own business," says Rosemary.

She's had to make some hefty sacrifices since starting her business, particularly financial ones. Her husband had to take on extra work and Rosemary herself would stay at work from 6:00 in the morning to 2:00 in the morning every single day, essentially forgoing sleep. But her vision includes having the courage to commit and persevere through any challenges and failures she may face.

In 2009, Rosemary was forced to put her business on hold when she discovered she had a brain tumor. Through seven surgeries and countless resulting side effects for her to deal with, the dream that got her through was one of someday re-opening her business. "I finally was able to start up again in 2011," she says. "I just have to keep working hard, leveling up, and being unafraid to ask for help." She recalls how she was able to use her experience to help a customer of hers who also had brain cancer.

"We just connected and we supported each other," she says. "All it took was a few minutes of talking with her to make a difference in someone's life." She realizes that in moments of generosity, it's important to do it with your heart in the right place and without rushing. She knows the value of taking things slowly and never giving up. "Your turning points don't have to end as failures," says Rosemary. For her, the best way to move forward is to address her own shortcomings head-on.

**"I've found that the one thing that helps me live peacefully and mindfully on this glorious planet is successful meaningful work--keeping my mind where my hands are, continuing to work hard at what I love no matter what the odds are."**

# Sheena Lyles

## Queen Foreverrr

Sheena Lyles was Facebooking one day when she stumbled upon a video of a comedian named King Bach that ignited a research spree where she sought out all the deaf comedians she could. "No successful Black Deaf comediennes existed," she says, "so I thought it was time for me to step up and learn how I could make people laugh." Her first post got a high number of views and likes, which intrigued and inspired Sheena, who began posting more and more.

Soon she started up her own YouTube channel and started making videos regularly, taking painful or annoying experiences and turning them into funny stories to share. Sheena considers her most notable accomplishment to be getting herself onstage as a comedian at the Deaf Women of Color Conference. In addition, she has acted in a TV One show called For My Woman as Daphne Wright, and makes a point of discussing the importance of accurate representations of Black Deaf women on screen and otherwise.

"There aren't as many people of color in comedy, and even fewer women of color," she notes. It's vital to her to have their experiences shared and represented correctly. "What gets to me is when people complain if a someone talks 'too much' about being a woman, black, deaf," says Sheena. "It's like, 'Yeah, sometimes we talk about it because that's a big part of how we experience life.'" She personally loves bringing up race and Deaf and hearing people in her comedy often because she's very interested in people and how we interact with one another. "Everyone can relate to these things because we have to deal with it on a daily basis," she says, "whether consciously or unconsciously."

One thing her business can't live without? "If I want to reveal my secret, I need to see some I.D. first," she quips, before admitting her DSLR camera is her secret weapon. Her life partner is another huge asset, fully supporting her through the ups and downs. "I was idle for a couple months, not making anything, because depression struck me hard," she says. "The more I focused on my comedy, the more I was afraid I wasn't good enough." Sheena worried that people would no longer think she was funny, or that they would laugh at her rather than with her. But Sheena's partner wouldn't stand for the self-doubt, and motivated her to get back into creating comedy videos once again.

"I love editing the videos, having others open up to me, having fans share their funny experiences with me," she says. Although she admits that editing and captioning her videos can be excruciatingly challenging as well, her hands flying to try to capture the exciting visions in her brain--seeing her audience laugh is something she holds dear to her heart, for it makes it all worth it.

**"For me, sharing my Light means helping others come out of their caves."**

# Melissa Malzkuhn

## Ink & Salt, Deaf Youth USA, Motion Light Lab

When she was ten years old, Melissa ma's grandfather brought her to an art store. He explained each item's purchase, watching her fascination with all the supplies, before buying a compartmental art case. "We left the store and he turned and said, 'This is for you,' and handed me the case," Melissa remembers. That day, her ten-year-old self was transformed. "I was no longer dealing with basic pencils," she says. "I had pastels, oil-based colored pencils, special erasers, and an art case to put everything in. I knew I would be an artist."

Today, Melissa is a storyteller, creative advocate, pioneer, and innovator. She is inspired by a quote she read in an interview with *Game of Thrones* creator George R. R. Martin. "Ideas are cheap," he said. "It's the execution of them that really counts." For her, it means that anyone can generate ideas, but nothing beats the art of doing. "It's always hard, complicated, impossible," she notes. "But we've got to go forward and *do*."

She's unfazed by the challenge of moving forward, no matter where she may end up along the way. She is the manager of Digital Innovations & Media Strategies, and the founder and creative director of the Motion Light Lab, at Gallaudet University. Melissa is also the founder of Deaf Youth USA and Ink & Salt. The first is an organization for Deaf youth aged 18-35, intended to promote social activism and social justice. Ink & Salt, her other brainchild, is a creative productions company that's responsible for The ASL App, a tool to teach people conversational ASL.

At one point, Melissa found herself feeling stagnant and decided to embark on a new quest, which led her to join the inaugural class of the School of Visual Arts' MFA in Visual Narrative. She recognizes nothing happens overnight and stresses the value of patience; she is passionate about always bringing her ideas to fruition. In her work with the Motion Light Lab, a space where creative literature and digital technology intersect to create immersive learning experiences, Melissa has helped create six ASL and English storybook apps. She compares walking into a creative zone like walking into the Light. "It's always passion that guides me through projects," says Melissa. "My motivation is to create experiences, things, ideas--that that transcend boundaries of languages and cultures to touch on human empathy."

**"Sharing my Light means absolute belief in myself, and by believing in the inevitable connection of things, the Universe simply unfolds."**

92

# Marlee Matlin

## Academy Award Winning Actor

Marlee Matlin wears many different hats. She is an actor, an advocate, an activist, an author, a producer, and a mother to four children. It's quite fitting then that as a child, she used to sit in front of the mirror and act out as many different roles as she could think of. She'd make up songs and monologues as a nun, a nurse, a salesperson, garbage truck driver--you name it, she wanted to try it out. "My mother would smile and nod as she watched me, but she wanted me to do something more productive than sit in front of a mirror and talk to myself," Marlee laughs. "So I got involved in what was known as the International Center on Deafness and the Arts in Chicago, auditioned for their first show, *The Wizard of Oz*, and the rest is history."

The legendary "history" that Marlee's referring to is, of course, the Academy Award she won for her role as Sarah Norman in the film adaptation of Children of a Lesser God just a few years later. As the first Deaf actor to ever win an Oscar--and the youngest winner of the Best Actress category still today--Marlee exploded into prominence in the Deaf community overnight and at 21 years old, became the most well-known Deaf person worldwide. Marlee recalls how humbling it was to receive the call about the nomination while in a drug rehabilitation center she had checked herself into after filming, a moment that inspired the title of her autobiography, I'll Scream Later.

She stands by her decision to become sober at 21, noting it as her proudest accomplishment. "That gave me clarity. It allowed me to take a hard look at who I was and be truly honest," she says. Although being the iconic face of the Deaf community brought its own battles, she's come to embrace the balance between heeding criticism from the public and standing in her truth. "People have many different perceptions of me...it was a rollercoaster for many years, but at the same time, I was learning too," says Marlee. "Then I realized I needed to learn about myself before everyone else does." The years since have found her on countless film and television sets, nominated for four Emmys and a slew of other awards, and brightening the lives of masses of individuals around the world. Today, she is involved with many different causes and charities and is particularly passionate about working with children to improve their lives.

As a mother of four, one of her biggest sacrifices over the years has been time with her kids, particularly having to miss significant moments in their lives. She'll never forget her son's first day of kindergarten, when she asked her boss at The West Wing if they'd mind if she came into work an hour later that Monday so she could drop off her son. They said no. "Missing milestones like that have been a huge sacrifice for me," she says. "But it is what it is. You commit yourself to something, you have to stay committed." That fierce tenacity and a permanent feeling of gratitude have been the root of her strength through the tumultuous years, fulfilling her sense of self whether she is breaking barriers or simply being Marlee.

**"When there is Light, there is absolute generosity for others."**

# Lori Maynard

## CelebratesSouls

At a very young age, Lori embraced a connection with spirits and her own spirituality. The very first encounter she can recall is one with an angel who appeared in her bedroom, shining bright with a vibrant white light. To her surprise, she wasn't afraid. Her heart told her that she was being watched over, and questions began surfacing in her mind: *Why am I here? What is my purpose here on Earth?* From that experience, she realized she had the gifts of intuition and empathy.

As she grew older, her fear of being perceived as outlandish stifled her intuitive gifts, and though her soul tugged at her not to, she chose to ignore her calling. After a teacher told her she couldn't chase her dreams of being an earth scientist, historian, or an anthropologist, a discouraged Lori ironically decided to become a teacher herself. She taught ASL and interpreting programs for 25 years before finally finding an opportunity to reconnect with her spirituality. "I realized I wanted to give back to the community," she says. "There's a market for Deaf people who are hungry to learn more about spirituality."

It was a huge financial sacrifice in order to build her business, but Lori was willing to give up her job in order to build her dream. Lori's business transformation coach, Sofia Seitchik, encouraged her to start the business with her passion for teaching in mind, and CelebrateSouls was actualized. Her company's purpose is to share the experience of spirituality and help people get in touch with their own life's purpose through intuition, astral travel, akashic records, tree-hugging classes, and other spiritual tools. "I wanted to provide access to these services for the Deaf community," she says, "to help them awaken their souls and understand who they are so that they may know their journey."

One tough barrier is the rapidly advancing technological aspect of business. "I'm clueless with technology, but I contact friends and I'm open about what I need in asking them for help," she says. Language also plays a role in causing complications during business interactions. "I was afraid people would misunderstand me, that I wouldn't be aware of their tone or understand hearing culture," she says. "But I realized I'm human. I just have to keep going, regardless of imperfections."

In moments when she needs motivation, Lori looks to her mentors and her wife, Jean, for support. "You can't worry about what people think of you, and you can't sit and wait for magic to happen," she says. She focuses instead on being a Light to others; in her words, bringing beauty, vibrancy, energy, power, love, and peace to others. "I really enjoy doing one-on-one training," says Lori. "Seeing them open up, finally awake. They've found who they are."

**"Open with love and let the Light come to you so you can share your Light with others. Love is a powerful tool."**

# Dr. Candace McCullough & Sharon Duchesneau

## Deaf Counseling Center

When non-signers took over management positions for a local community agency where Dr. Candace McCullough was working as the director of Deaf mental health services, she resolved to leave that oppressive work environment, obtain her PhD, and start her business, Deaf Counseling Center, with her life partner--Sharon Duchesneau.

At the time, Sharon was working part-time while taking care of their daughter. It made sense for them to work together, and now they're co-running a Deaf-centered counseling practice specializing in providing services to Deaf clients all over the country. "We believe that Deaf people have the right to accessible counseling," says Sharon. "They shouldn't have to worry about interpreters, privacy, or explaining Deaf culture during their sessions." Deaf Counseling Center is the very first Deaf women-owned counseling business that makes it possible for Deaf people all over the United States to receive counseling through videophone as well as in-person services.

It's not always easy for them to run their business together primarily from their shared home. "I don't have the luxury of separating my work and home lives. I've had to learn to become comfortable with intertwining both of these areas in my life," says Candace. As for Sharon, she feels her biggest sacrifice is time. "Even though I save a lot of time by commuting downstairs to work," she jokes, "as our business has grown, so have the demands on my time." But as business partners and life partners, they are able to lean on one another for support, each crediting the other as her biggest supporter. It helps that they are ardently invested in the work they do as well. "The best thing of all is when you are doing what means something to you and makes you feel good," says Sharon. "I'm honored to be a part of my clients' lives."

"I love that clients teach me new things. Being a psychotherapist allows me to share so many intimate moments with clients," Candace says. Once, in eighth grade, she was told by her teacher that she couldn't be a lawyer like she wanted because the teacher didn't believe that Deaf people who didn't speak could be lawyers. "I would tell young Deaf girls wanting to pursue their own dreams to never take no for an answer! This," she cautions, "does not mean arguing forever with whoever tells you no. It means finding another way or finding a loophole that will allow you to make your dream a reality." Sharon agrees, adding that they shouldn't be intimidated by hearing people or even by men who may discourage them.

**"Helping people shine their Light makes the world brighter. Shining only my Light will not have as much of an impact." - Dr. Candace McCullough**

# Ann Meehan

## The Signing Group of Real Estate Teams

After buying her first house at 25, Ann Meehan fell in love with the thrill of making a deal. She has a penchant for real estate and has always loved houses. However, she focused on being at home and raising her two young daughters in Massachusetts, until her husband left the family. It was imperative to her not to rely on a man or anyone else for financial stability, so she made a bold move to start building up her own income. She found her moxie and moved to Washington, D.C. with her children to attend Gallaudet University, where she met her current husband and had another daughter, Michelle Lapides. Ann has five generations of deaf family members including deaf grandparents, parents, herself, two daughters, and her grandson. All come from different eras of communication access, and there are vast gaps in their experiences due to rapidly-changing technology. "It is fortunate for me knowing that my Deaf offspring became my Deaf role models," says Ann.

Ann grew up in high school without interpreters, when there were not many career options for deaf individuals. Her dad, one of her biggest supporters, always encouraged her by telling her she could do it, no matter what "it" was. It all began when Ann searched for a realtor that knew ASL to represent the sale of her fourth home. Next thing she knew, Ann got the opportunity to really jump into the world of real estate. She decided at 45 to start her business and pave her own way with The Signing Group of Real Estate Teams, which provides sign language access to real estate. The biggest challenges when Ann first started included embracing the expanding technological aspect of business never before present, and doubters questioning how a Deaf realtor would be able to negotiate a deal in a very competitive marketplace.

Her older daughters, Elizabeth Kalis-McGuire and Jennifer Kalis, who are also on the team, grew up accompanying Ann on tours of model homes. They watched her survive as a single, working mother and navigate the process of becoming a realtor, and it was important to Ann that they see a financially independent, career woman as an example. She believes that running a business requires good networking skills and also a strong team, which she has in her daughters. In 2016, The Signing Group hit ten million dollars of sales in that year alone.

"A home is the most important place in anybody's life," she says. "It is an asset and among the best investments anyone can make. However, buying or selling a home can be stressful." This is why Ann makes sure she is there every step of the way, making the process seamless and comfortable for everyone.

**"Always remember that life is freedom of choice. You have the power to choose what you want out of your life. Own it!"**

# Malene Malender

## *SexandLove*

Talking about sexual information is not easy for many people, but for Malene Melander, it is the essence of her career. When she was growing up, she wanted to be a psychologist, but she eventually became a teacher. During her work in education, she realized many Deaf kids were sexually abused by adults or by other Deaf kids in school or on the bus. "Because of this awful realization," she says, "I grew a heartfelt passion to teach sexual awareness to Deaf kids who were fluent in sign language."

She admits that sign language often presents an extra layer of challenge for people in teaching sexual health information. "When people discuss this topic in sign language, it is very graphic," she acknowledges. "Some teachers find it intimidating or uncomfortable to discuss, so they won't go into detail. But the result is that young Deaf children continue to lack information about sexual health and safety." While working as a teacher, she came to a point where she didn't know what she wanted and she was no longer able to feel herself. When the stress became too much, she collapsed. "I was fighting so hard to be the good girl, the best employee, and the perfect mother," she says. During her sick leave, she ended up meeting a great job coach who taught her the importance of being vulnerable.

"In my own healing process, I discovered a new passion," says Malene. "I wanted other women to feel free, just like I had experienced through different self-awareness courses." So after her time teaching at the Deaf school came to a close, she became a sexologist and a love coach. She now guides women, couples, and families on issues of communication, sexuality, and love.

"I love to teach women how to become whole, rather than perfect," says Malene. Residing in Denmark, she is the only Deaf business owner there who offers online products in sign language. At first, though, it was a struggle to get people to buy her services. "Being a certified sexologist doesn't mean you're trained to be a business owner," she says. "I got frustrated; I thought something was wrong with me." But Malene, with her steady character, wouldn't give up. She changed her dream into a plan: she studied everything there was to know about owning a business.

What she's learned is it takes time. "Every baby step in the right direction is a good step, no matter how small," she says. But she adds that it's important to start straightaway without allowing doubt to postpone your goals. "You will never know everything," she says. "You know enough--just start!"

**"Light is the way you communicate with your soul and find your own way of living fully with love, wholeness, joy, and balance."**

# Rebecca Moir

## *Glam by Becca*

Glam, radiant, and chic--that's how you can describe Rebecca Moir. She doesn't just beautify hair and faces, she opens a window to their souls as well. Cosmetology school was simply supposed to be a backup plan just in case, but she ended up falling in love with hair and makeup and turning it into her profession. "My mom is the one who got me into hairstyling as a career," Rebecca says, explaining that when doctors kept insisting that she was hearing, her mom took it upon herself to learn sign language in order to communicate with Rebecca. "She was my biggest cheerleader--she always said I could do anything I wanted." She now runs Glam By Becca, a mobile hairstyling business where she travels to clients' houses in order to provide services like haircuts, hair extensions, and keratin treatments.

"I live in a great community with a large number of Deaf residents, and I love that I can help them get their hair exactly how they want it," she says. "I'm able to communicate clearly with them and relate to them." She was working at a salon in Philadelphia a few years back before meeting her husband online and moving to Maryland to start a family with him. "After we had kids, I didn't want to go back to working in a salon," says Rebecca. Instead, she started offering her services to the other moms in her mothers' group and to their kids.

"I love making people feel good about themselves and boosting their self-esteem," she says. Reaching out to people and traveling to them is part of what she loves so much about Glam By Becca. "I've worked a lot of hours, but bringing Light into other people's lives and making sure my clients are fully happy with my services is so important to me!" says Rebecca. For her, it's wonderful having so many Deaf clients that she can communicate with and completely understand, but she doesn't underestimate the patience and passion required in starting up any business.

"You have to have faith in yourself. I did whatever I could to get my name and my business out there," she says. Rebecca now has a full book and continues to throw "Hair Parties" for groups of women for various events. "I only wish I had done this much sooner," she laughs. In the end, it was her childhood passion that turned into her profession--showing that it's often the first desires that are your truest passions.

**"Light shines out there by the work I put into my clients, and by making my clients feel worthy and lifting them inside out!"**

# Sarah Morrison

## Protactile Connects

Sarah Morrison remembers fighting with her mother every morning because she absolutely dreaded going to school. As a Deaf child without any interpreters or peers to facilitate support, she often felt isolated and lost in the classroom. She recalls an assignment in third grade where the students had to concoct a report on what they wanted to be when they grew up, and she struggled with the concept because of her lack of access to language. "I saw another student write the word banker, and on an impulse, I wrote it down too," she says. "Even though I had no idea what that meant." On the picture taken by her teacher, the word banker was written when it really should have read lost, according to Sarah.

She remembers the years of adversity as she felt like she was losing herself, becoming blind in college and being unable to find a full-time job as a DeafBlind person. The more challenges she takes on, however, the more she cultivates her resilience and inner strength. "Taking myself out of my comfort zone provides me with a chance to grow personally and professionally," she says. "Practicing yoga and surrounding myself with positive energy has helped." Sarah now has a rich resume chock-full of her various experiences advocating for and working with the DeafBlind community. "It is significant that no one gets left behind," she affirms, "to encourage inclusion, not isolation--and to make sure everyone is accommodated." It's important to her to foster a community that has equal access to language, resources, networking, and information.

Sarah currently works as a freelance consultant, providing training on ProTactile and access for the DeafBlind community, as many people are isolated with no way of getting information or resources. To help other DeafBlind individuals stimulate a sense of pride in their identities, she also encourages others to host ProTactile social nights for the community to convene. "This has been an opportunity to make changes," says Sarah. "To share the passion, knowledge, love...in order to do that, one must first feel free." Her goal is to educate people on what it means to be wholesome, experiencing all dualities of life and rediscovering their freedom.

"Finding those who share the same passion is how we achieve the goal of working together as a community," she says. "It takes a community to make things happen, to make an impact, and to bring about awareness." Sarah finds strength in having an attitude of trust and optimism that everything will work out one way or another. "Ultimately, it's your choice in how to keep moving forward in life."

**"When I joined yoga, I would often remind myself: be the Light. Breathe in love, breathe out fear; breathe in compassion, breathe out enmity; breathe in hope, breathe out doubt; breathe in resilience, breathe out frustration. Trust all will be okay."**

# Dawnena Michelle Muth

## *Dreamgivers*

When Dawnena Michelle Muth and her sister were growing up, they would often play office. "It was in the days of that famous commercial where a woman was singing, 'I can bring home the bacon and fry it in a pan,' and we saw a woman who could do it all!" says Dawnena. "We learned women could make a difference in the office *and* in the household." From there, she aspired to be a business executive, but soon came to the realization she had been living her life for other people--and hit rock bottom. However, she drew upon the strength of the women in her family in order to pick up the pieces of herself she had lost.

"My grandmother, whom I am named after, raised five children; my mother has had her own business since I was seven years old," says Dawnena. "I've watched both my mother and sister run their own businesses while going through every challenge life handed them." So when she hit her low point, she knew she had to take everything they'd taught her and change something in order to follow what she believed was best for her.

It was then that she turned to her spirituality in order to better connect with herself and her Native American culture. Enrolled in the tribe of Pawnee Nation, Dawnena was taught that we shine our Lights just like the stars from whence we came. She found value and greatness within that she hadn't felt before, and had a vision that her calling is to unite the Deaf and hearing worlds. "I believe I am called to be a peacemaker," she says. During a business mastermind group, she came across advice from author Jack Canfield: *take 100% responsibility of yourself.* "I took a long, hard look at myself," she says. "I owned up to what was happening around me."

Then came Dreamgivers, the company Dawnena started in order to provide business coaching to those who need guidance--but she often goes deeper than business. "Make sure you focus on personal development," she advises. She insists that having a plan, a vision, and a journal is absolutely essential to starting and running your own business. "I got a journal and wrote down everything years ago--my wishes are now coming to fruition," she says. Although she's struggled with finances in the past, especially as a single mother to four children, she took responsibility by recently paying off everything she owed.

Dawnena is extremely passionate about encouraging others to see that their dreams can come true. "Some do not know their value in this world," she says. For them, seeing how she overcame so many barriers in her life helps them see the Light in her. "We are all Light in a dark world, and shining your Light means you are spreading love to those who are in the dark," she says. "Everyone is looking for hope. When we shine, we are showing them that hope exists."

**"I wish I knew that it only takes me to start believing in myself."**

# Irina Miriam Normatov

## The Wealth of Joy

Irina Normatov took her first flight when she was just three years old. She flew thousands of miles from her hometown in Samarkand, Uzbekistan to St. Petersburg, Russia, where she spent the next six years in a boarding school for the deaf with her older sister Sofia--only going back in the summers to see her hearing parents and other sisters. "I would lie awake at night in the daycare all alone, not yet in the same school with Sofia as we were seven years apart," she says. Her almond brown eyes and black hair were a stark contrast to the blue and blond of the peers who outcasted her.

Even when her family immigrated to the melting pot that is New York City, nine-year-old Irina couldn't quite come to terms with her identity as a Deaf Bukharian Jewish girl. Connecting with her identity was a constant struggle; she thought she would never feel joy and freedom in her heart. The cultural conflicts and language barriers within her traditional family didn't make things easier. "I wanted to break every rule," says Irina, who finally began to discover herself better through her interactions with people from all walks of life. As her mind expanded its horizons to understand their pains and joys, she navigated her way to becoming an empath. The minute she changed the way she was thinking of herself and others, something shifted overnight--as if ropes around her were released, unknotting her soul from the darkness. "By believing and trusting in who I am and accepting the circumstances of my life, my layers of blockage and limited mindset were set free," she says. Ever since this profound epiphany, intuition has been the guiding force of her life.

"When I found my intuitive skills, I found my confidence," remarks Irina. She cultivated so much from her experiences with people's behavior and mindsets, leaping through different careers--as an Events and Marketing Consultant, the Northeast District Manager of a Video Relay Service company, and the Creative Liaison Director of Global Deaf Women. In conversations, her intuition would reveal insights about the other person, which she would share with them to help them see their Light or understand their next move. Those same instincts soon paved her path to her own business--The Wealth of Joy.

Influenced by her inner gifts, Irina engages her clients with workshops, consulting their choice of thoughts, shifting mindsets, and expanding the possibilities that lead them to their Light. Her dream is to create a platform to share stories of Deaf humans; their experiences, their struggles, their breakthroughs. "Because I was a disconnected soul one too many times," she explains, "healing people with the awareness of joy has become my passion." For Irina, seeing an individual realize the worth of their being and find their way to fulfilling joy and deeper understanding of the power of life is a gift.

**"Light sparkles when I am naturally joyful and deeply connected to my soul and Universe; my heart rhymes in the drum of the beats like good music."**

# Gina Pasini

## Charmeleonized Ones

Growing up Deaf in a hearing family, Gina Pasini often had no one to talk to at holiday gatherings. After she finished her dinner, she would sneak under the table and snatch her uncle's camera so she wasn't bored out of her mind sitting there at a big, white, lace-covered table. As soon as her uncle would catch her taking pictures with his camera, she'd have to give it back--but not without pouting. Without the camera, she would draw pictures with cranberry sauce and paint with a milk-filled straw on her napkin.

After giving birth to her first child, a talent she had little explored came to light. The moment Gina saw her son and his adorable strands of hair sticking out, she knew that the image was fleeting. She had an urge to take a photo and captured his picture in a way nobody had ever seen before. Gina brings light to things we look at everyday and makes people appreciate them in a different perspective.

Gina considers herself a survivalist, and always tells herself that she has to keep swimming and explore every opportunity. Indeed, the rainbow--the good--always comes after the storm--the worst She reminds herself that everything happens for a reason, and it is all about timing. If the door is closed, she moves onto a different path. Life is never scripted.

Today, Gina is an unique artist; painting, crafting, and quilting. She does anything out of the ordinary, and according to her, it comes from a forgotten childhood and having grown up "the different one." Since diving into her calling, Gina has opened an Etsy shop; hung twelve wood artwork panels at Deaf-owned San Francisco pizzeria, Mozzeria; had a dream-created quilt featured in a special Best Modern Quilts of 2014 issue; and had an Instagram pillowcase art piece featured in the *San Francisco Chronicle*.

Among all her successes, Gina has found that the biggest challenge in her business is communicating with and resolving disputes professionally with a wide variety of customers from all over the world in her third language--English. She also finds it challenging to finish products within a specific timeframe, as she is a single mother of three children. Gina has had to make some sacrifices in terms of time away from her children.

Gina's childhood escapades grew into the business she calls Charmeleonized Ones--a name as unique as she is. Her passion for her art is the best fuel for her creativity, and she encourages young Deaf women to know exactly who they are because no one can tell them who they are or what they can do.

**"Just keep swimming, in a shallow creek or a wavy ocean; you'll find treasures, small or big--only you can jigsaw them into your dreams."**

"Don't become a victim of your

circumstances...

use them as stepping stones."

Claudia Lorraine Gordon

# Joette Paulone

## Filming PAH

Staring at her beautiful long-haired dolls, a young Joette Paulone held her mom's scissors in her hand before promptly chopping off all their hair. "I didn't like that they had no soul," she says. "I wanted to make them show facial expressions so I could play with them, and I thought a haircut might work." After receiving only stoic faces in response, Joette took her scissors to her next client: her sister.

"The first time, she ended up with bald spots," Joette admits. But her sister, who had dealt with headaches all her life and loved the head massage that came with her haircut, took it with a smile. Her family members could see the Light in Joette's heart as she practiced on them, encouraging her to keep going and grow in her confidence. She ran her first salon out of her parents' basement in Philadelphia, and she enjoyed a successful 15-year career before moving to Maryland for her Deaf sons' education. There, she faced the same challenges she faced in Pennsylvania--the cosmetology school refusing to provide interpreters, even as she fought tirelessly. Finally, she decided her belief in herself was enough. She attended and finished school with no interpreters.

Joette then received a grant from the state of Maryland to open her own beauty shop while she was with her moribund father in the hospital. But in the midst of his passing, she ended up missing the deadline. Tragedy struck once more the next time she successfully applied for a grant. This time, it was her mother who passed away, and Joette lost the grant when she rushed home to care for her sister. This, however, led her to a job in the drama department at Maryland School for the Deaf, where she taught students how to style hair while simultaneously working as a freelance hairstylist. Because she could empower students while styling hair, it ended up being a fantastic 20-year career. As a Deaf woman who grew up in the age of oralism, Joette fondly recalls the dorms where she and other girls could sign freely and take turns telling stories, encouraging each other in their creativity.

Today, Joette is a co-partner of Filming PAH as well as an experienced performer, acting in and directing several works of theatre in Colorado. She notes that the struggles with accessibility she's faced throughout her life have blessed her with being able to turn negatives into positives. She encourages young Deaf girls today to have a strong passion for whatever dreams they pursue.

**"With every barrier I face, my Light breaks through to the right path once more."**

# Karen Putz

## Ageless Passions

Before Karen Putz was the successful writer, passion mentor, speaker, and the all-around Renaissance woman she is today, she was a beginner. Her dream as a child was to be an author like Danielle Steel or write for the *Chicago Tribune* like Erma Bombeck, but at 44 she found herself working in a ho-hum job as a sales manager.

After losing her dad to cancer and being let go from the company around the same time, she decided it was high time to do what she really loved to do: write. She used the time afterward to write several books and even wrote articles for the Chicago Tribune like she had always wanted. In the midst of rediscovering her passion for writing, she found a passion for helping others do exactly that--find their passions.

Today Karen is known as the Passion Mentor and runs a business called Ageless Passions where she helps others discover how to live passion-infused lives. She emphasizes the importance of having a strong network around you and investing financially in your own self-development, even when the sacrifice is difficult.

One thing she wishes she had known before she dove passionately into the world of business is that every successful person starts out as a beginner first. "You can't compare your beginning steps with someone else's end point of success," notes Karen. Having a strong mentor on your side is also highly valuable. "But if there's something you want to do that's never been done, maybe you have to be the one to lead the way," Karen says.

This former beginner certainly knows a thing or two about leading the way. In her teens, she learned how to barefoot waterski and was the only girl barefooting in a gaggle of men on the lake for years. After going deaf at 19 from a hard fall, she gave up the sport in favor of immersing herself in the world of ASL and becoming a mom. At 44, she finally picked up the old ski handle again and found her passion once more, which ignited her love for helping others find their passions and their own inner Light.

**"Light is your brilliance, your uniqueness. In the whole wide world, there is *no one* just like you. Shine on. When we shine our light on others, we illuminate the other person as well."**

# Rajarajeshwari

## Deafhood Yoga

The light of yoga has always been present throughout Rajarajeshwari's life. However, it wasn't until several bouts of trauma in 2000 that she finally embraced the holistic health approach, fully understanding the connection between a yogic path and living as a whole being. "I always evoked strong positive responses in healing whenever I incorporated the five petals of yoga: pranayama, relaxation, asanas, lifestyle, and meditation," shares Rajarajeshwari. "Yoga teaches us to live in harmony with ourselves, everyone, and everything."

As an empath, she was fascinated by the strong connections she feels with all paths of spirituality, especially with Buddhism, Deafhood, Hinduism, and Native American ideology. "To me, the word Deafhood means the consciousness of sharing a similar experience growing up as a Deaf person, like childhood, sisterhood, motherhood, and so on," says Rajarajeshwari. "It's also a journey that each Deaf person undertakes to discover their true identity and purpose here on Earth."

Her own journey led her to a quote from Dr. Paddy Ladd's book, *Understanding Deaf Culture: In Search of Deafhood*, that inspired her: "Deafhood is a process to decolonize our mind, body, and spirit from colonization." She realized the oppression the Deaf community undergoes fosters a survival instinct, inspiring a path for healing--a similar path of healing, Rajarajeshwari noted, that yoga provides. Suddenly, she received a powerful vision of the parallels between Deafhood and yoga. Her marriage of the two spiritual journeys manifested as Deafhood Yoga, an online studio where people all over the world can experience the multidimensional light of Deaf-centered yoga through ASL.

According to Rajarajeshwari, Deafhood and yoga are both a personal process: a union of the higher self, communities, and the Universe. "Deafhood and yoga liberate us to just be," she says. As she teaches in Deafhood Yoga, the Lotus reminds human beings to rise above all the negativity, drama, and the ego of the mind through vibrant love. The unfolding of its leaves is symbolic of detachment as droplets of water slide easily off its petals, expanding the soul and igniting a spiritual awakening.

Rajarajeshwari's reawakening was interrupted by the sudden departure of her beloved father, which turned her life upside down. However, this only intensified her strength. "Faith means knowing it will happen even though I do not know how," she says. "My solar plexus chakra was then fueled into becoming a certified yoga and meditation teacher of all ages." Her aim in sharing the practice of yoga is to raise consciousness and compassion in order to reduce suffering in humanity worldwide. Her advice to young Deaf girls is to listen to their own inner Light, for only they know what their hearts beat for.

**"You are Light, I am Light, and We are Light."**

# Rezenet Moges Riedel

## *University Lecturer*

Rezenet Moges Riedel's childhood dream was to become either a firefighter or Indiana Jones. "I achieved the latter one," she laughs. "I spent eight years as an Archaeological Graphics Director and realized that it wasn't quite the dream I was envisioning." Although the discoveries her team made were fascinating, she felt she was not contributing enough to Deaf academia. The child in her had no idea she was a linguistic anthropologist at heart and would end up becoming a professor just like her dad.

Her turning point came when one of her closest colleagues recognized her frustration at not being able to give back to the Deaf community, and he invited her to sit in and momentarily take over his class. "I was viciously bitten by the teaching bug," she says. Rezenet has taught at three different community colleges and is now a full-time lecturer at California State University, Long Beach, where she is assisting with their new ASL Linguistics and Deaf Cultures program. That frustration she'd felt instantly disappeared once students showed their profound gratitude for how much they had learned from her courses at the end, to their own surprise.

Early on she was advised, if she didn't see her identity represented enough, to become that somebody who puts their marginalized group back on the map and creates the necessary changes in society. As a queer Deaf woman and daughter of immigrants whose family emigrated from Eritrea in Africa, she seized her opportunity to step in by giving lectures based on experiences with her intersectional background. She was frequently worried about her queer identity, wondering if it would tarnish her family's reputation in their African diaspora community. "But in order to be that 'somebody,' I know I need to look forward without constantly peering over my shoulder," says Rezenet.

She is a contributing author to four different volumes; two books published by Gallaudet University Press, and the other two by De Gruyter Mouton and Oxford University Press. Her publications focus on topics such as Crip Theory in Deaf/Disability Studies, stressing the significance of intersectionality in one's disability identity and their other identities. "The most exciting thing is that we are now moving in a direction that is more centered on Deaf-plus and indigenous identities for scholarships," she says. This enables each marginalized group to bring in their own perspectives and broaden the conversation to include people from all backgrounds. Rezenet also describes herself as an ASL poet and occasional artist. Her printmaking art and oil paintings were displayed at RIT and CSUN's art galleries for Black and People of Color Deaf artists' exhibitions, respectively.

**"I learned from my most influential figures, my parents: sharing your success with others, you'll elevate your communities to a higher ground and seize more opportunities together."**

# Jesica Zoe Rodriguez Melendez

## JeZoé for a Happy Skin

Jésica Zoé Rodríguez Meléndez, originally from Isabela, Puerto Rico, was reading an article about health, diet, and skin when she realized she could change and control her skin, if she only took the time to understand what was in the products she was using. So she got to work and began studying, citing advice from her teacher about the importance of buying Fair Trade Certified™ ingredients that were eco-friendly. Soon after taking courses on making natural saponified soaps, she was creating her own handmade soaps.

Upon receiving compliments from her delighted family members, she began selling her handmade soaps. She recalls one of her first customers--a mother whose son had suffered from eczema. A year later, Jésica met that same woman again, and the mom explained how her son's skin had gotten better using her soap. "What got me was the fact that she previously had tried various doctors, prescriptions, and even natural remedies," she said. "I was truly touched and proud."

Her biggest challenge, however, is communicating with hearing customers in order to sell them her products. She took all her classes without interpreters and succeeded in running her own business alone, even though she feels overwhelmed with frustration at times. Be it making soap, labeling, printing, packaging, or sending letters, she does it all on her own. Whenever she's experiencing moments of self-doubt, she gets momentum from taking a break and surrounding herself with nature. "When I see trees, I feel like they renew my positive energy. My purpose is to spread that positive energy to other people," says Jésica.

Her favorite part of spreading her joyful ambiance is being able to help people heal their skin problems. Jésica strives to be an honest, ethical business owner, and she advises young deaf women to always have the "I CAN" mentality. "The key thing in pursuing your dream is to get away from negative people," she said. "Don't focus on them." Instead, she chooses to focus on her own vision: how to best serve and educate people on getting healthier skin.

**"Sharing and shining my light is very important because it's a synergistic effect; I love sharing and receiving positive energy and happiness with everybody."**

# Jacqueline "Jackie" Roth

## *Licensed Associate Real Estate Broker*

Growing up as a child of Deaf parents, Jacqueline "Jackie" Roth found a role as a facilitator of sorts between the Deaf and hearing communities. She was a natural storyteller and easily fell into her passion for acting; however, she couldn't make a living at it. "I got into real estate after 9/11, after a series of difficult life changes," Jackie recalls. "I was broke and running out of savings. I knew I had to do something." Her motivation to find a new calling was mainly financial, in order to continue living in the upscale, bustling city of New York.

"Coming from a Deaf family and growing up without any knowledge or ties into the business world, it was baptism by fire," Jackie says. Her first year in real estate was endless learning, reading, and taking classes, but she finally got her first deal with a Deaf customer who took a chance on her because he wanted to understand what he was getting himself into and be engaged in the process. Being able to sign away with her Deaf customers when working with other brokers is very rewarding for Jackie. "Not a word is missed if I can help it," she promises.

Currently, Jackie is one of the top producers with one of the best real estate brokerages, Douglas Elliman, in the ultra-competitive New York City. "Being part of this company, I have the opportunity to dream the dreams of architects and developers," she says. "It's so much fun to view apartments and take in beautiful designs firsthand, because there is so much appreciation for the aesthetics." True to her artistic nature, she finds quite a few opportunities for creativity in her work. She considers the many phases of preparing to sell a property to be almost like staging a play. "It's like the theater for me, getting everything put together and ready for opening night--the open house," she says.

Jackie has now come to nurture the strong business acumen she wishes she had started out with and enjoys the time she invests in her clients. "I love that my work is about relationships, about helping my clients achieve their dreams...I'm constantly meeting new people outside of my comfort zone and learning new things," says Jackie, who considers herself a perpetual student.

She has also been a key player through decades of revolutionizing changes in the Deaf community, using media as a vehicle. Jackie has worked with attorneys on civil rights cases defining negligence and developed various training modules to be used in medical and legal settings. Her proudest public relations effort, however, was the Deaf President Now movement. In addition, Jackie has produced the Academy Award-nominated film, *Sound and Fury*. "I still have dreams," she says. "And I think that in itself is both an achievement and a challenge."

**"Never give in to the *nos* or *can'ts* when you know deep down it's what you want."**

# Nancy Rourke
## *The Expressionist Paintings*

Ever since Nancy Rourke was a child, she recognized her desire to be an artist, but knew how difficult it would be to make a living as a full-time artist who is Deaf. So for years she suppressed her pain into her art privately, until she discovered her turning point in the form of the book *Understanding Deaf Culture: In Search of Deafhood*. Nancy had an awakening. From there on out, she felt called and inspired to represent the collective Deaf history by painting her experiences and to help others explore their own Deafhood journey.

Her parents discovered she was deaf at six years old and consequently placed her in an oral program where she was forbidden to sign, as was the custom at the time. "I was caught doing what comes naturally to us Deaf children--signing--and as punishment, I was put into a small, dark closet," she says. After listening to many similar stories from her Deaf friends, she realized the Deaf community has a collective and cultural memory, a history of shared wounds. When she first picked up the paintbrush to begin healing those wounds, she finally cast away the doubt that had trapped her for so long. "Deafhood is what kept me going in the beginning; seeing De'VIA paintings, all of the experiences of resistance and affirmation," says Nancy. "So much of what I've achieved has been about taking risks in trial and error." She is so happy she made the leap to being a full-time artist like she always knew she wanted.

Nancy's hallmark is her use of only three colors in her artwork--red, yellow, and blue. "I was searching for a style. I was trying to come up with something that can get people to recognize my work. For a while, I was struggling with pigment green color. It never seemed to work well for me, and I decided to omit it," says Nancy. After just a few years of using primary colors and black and white, with her distinctive style and Deaf-experience focus, some artists called her style Rourkeism. Nancy considers it a humbling honor to have an recognizable Deaf-centered art style be named after her.

Nancy has come a long way since that dark closet. She considers each painting a brave visual of the truth for all to see, a testimony of sorts for the Deaf community's history. Sometimes it is quite intense, grueling, even heartbreaking. "All that I've done has been a labor of love. Love for my parents, however misguided, love for myself, and love for my community," says Nancy. "Art allows us to really feel that love."

**"We all need to be reminded to love--to love ourselves, each other, our culture, our language, our people, and our heritage."**

# Nicki Runge

## ImaginASL Performing Arts

Nicki Runge has never strayed from her original dream of becoming an actress, although she's now expanded her repertoire to include directing and producing. "I can't live without arts onstage," she says. Her ultimate vision is to produce ASL plays that can be enjoyed simultaneously by Deaf and hearing audiences alike. One of her biggest sacrifices along her journey was needing to simply jump in and push herself the whole way.

Nicki was inspired by theaters like Deaf West and National Theatre of the Deaf to start her own. With no ASL theaters or Deaf theatre programs in the Midwest, Nicki opened her first for-profit business, Rocky Mountain Deaf Theatre, in Colorado, where she was involved in creating plays to be performed in ASL. After five years, she decided to transfer her business into a nonprofit organization, and ImaginASL Performing Arts was manifested for Deaf and hearing audience members. In the middle of the process, she birthed her daughter prematurely, devoting much of her time to being in the neonatal intensive care unit. "I feel like that was my lowest point," says Nicki. "But my wonderful Deaf friends and allies in Colorado kept pushing, motivating me until I could pull myself up and help ImaginASL grow."

Her goal was to give the community more influence in playmaking so she could step back and bring on more actors, simultaneously enriching their experience and enabling her to spend more time with her daughter. She encouraged her board to close Rocky Mountain Deaf Theatre, and eventually her persistence paid off when it became ImaginASL at last. By getting the community more involved in different shows and children's plays through networking and fundraising, Nicki was able to expand her company and soon people were raving, excited about the collaboration between the hearing and Deaf worlds. "I started alone with an open mind, growing and building on the support of all the people I met," she says. When she first started out, her mentor advised her to "keep climbing the Everest" until she reached the top, where she is meant to be. "After five years of not giving up, I feel like I've hit the top of Everest," says Nicki.

She considers being able to balance her schedule as a mother and business owner an essential skill for running a company. "I try to take one or two days off every week to enjoy some quality time with my daughter and husband," she says. However, her passion for her vision helps to keep her focused on accomplishing her goals. She especially loves working with others who share the same goals or believe in the dream she's trying to put forth, but she also acknowledges that it's nice to have an aspiration just for yourself. "My advice for young Deaf girls is to focus on your passions no matter what, and ignore your friends' opinions if they don't share your goals and aren't interested in them," says Nicki.

**"Follow the soul in your heart; it will guide you where you want to go."**

# Terrylene Sacchetti

## ASL Poet and Actor

As an ASL poet, Terrylene Sacchetti applies the fundamentals of the language in captivating poetry with definitive forms that command the space. Her poetry evokes emotions through rhythmic movement, shifting shapes, compelling themes, and cinematic language, like images that move by in the frames of a film. Terrylene's face, body, and hands invite one to imagine and to be changed. Ultimately, the creations she stirs with her hands guide one through a mystical journey of the human spirit.

As a young girl, Terrylene often retreated to the bathroom to create poetry and perform in front of the mirror. It was her way of coping with a deep secret she didn't know how to reveal to anyone--she was sexually abused and she relied on her imagination as a tool for survival. Later as an adult, when she was able to reveal the truth, she leaned on her creativity once more to help herself heal. From her silence, she built a one-woman show, "In the Now," that went on a two-year tour. It gave a voice to organizations for Deaf women and children who have experienced violence or abuse.

Nowadays, she does poetry anywhere and anytime, whenever she feels the creativity swelling in her well. Audience or no audience, she simply creates. She feels she was always destined to be a poet. Acting is another powerful outlet of expression for Terrylene. Throughout her life, Terrylene appeared in numerous stage, film, and television productions, but often found the entertainment world limiting with little consideration for the diverse people in it. "The entertainment industry didn't--and still don't--fully appreciate nor understand ASL artistic expressions. I saw value in using my artwork to enhance the linguistic growth of Deaf children and their families," says Terrylene.

The best piece of advice she was given? When she auditioned for the lead role in a play at a regional theatre, her drama teacher simply said: "You gave your best. Now, forget about it." Terrylene understood that to mean, "Move on and keep creating." She did get the role and it ended up being a wonderful experience. While she's also had her fair share of tragic disappointments, she says they help her to understand just why she does what she does--they make her stronger. At her lowest points, Terrylene relies on grace to get through, and difficult times have also taught her to be kind to herself with acts of self-love. "Set up tools to comfort your soul, be it a hot bath, hot tea, or chocolate, writing in a journal, taking a walk through the trees, drawing pictures, or watching inspiring, jaw-dropping videos," she says. "They always lighten me up and give me hope. When you feel your deepest emotions, honor them then let them pass."

**"Kindness spreads like ripples in the water and stirs one's heart."**

# Sofia Normatov Seitchik

## Global Deaf Women

The woman with the vision. The muse with the inspiration. The entrepreneur with the purpose. Sofia Seitchik, certified life coach and businesswoman extraordinaire, is the engine behind Global Deaf Women. Her passion is helping women who are current or aspiring business owners in building their confidence, achieving their visions, and discovering their inner Light.

Born in Samarkand, Uzbekistan where opportunities for girls were extremely limited, Sofia was sent to a school for the deaf over 2,500 miles away in St. Petersburg, Russia when she was just three years old. Her mother was determined to help Sofia get access to a better education. The sacrifice of living so far away meant Sofia had to figure out everything virtually alone, with no role models to look up to. "It was most painful growing up without my family," says Sofia, who could only go back and see them during summer breaks. Though her childhood was peppered with vibrant cultures, languages, and experiences, it was her family's move to New York City when she was 16 that opened up her world further. Despite having no knowledge of English or ASL, she rolled up her sleeves and wrestled every obstacle in her way. "Arriving in the United States felt like an awakening," says Sofia. "The world was so much more accessible, and I had more opportunities than I had ever dreamed of, especially as a Deaf woman."

Early on after finishing college, Sofia landed her dream career as a Coordinator of Community Affairs. She loved her work, often attending motivational conferences and traveling on the side, but she felt something was missing. Meanwhile, since the conferences she went to were run by hearing people, she was growing frustrated by the lack of Deaf mentors, speakers, and attendees. She sought out Deaf motivational conferences so she could share her experiences with other Deaf people in her own language, but found nothing. This eye-opening revelation and her own arduous journey planted the seed for the formation of Global Deaf Women. Utilizing her inner gifts, she took the risk to quit her stable job with benefits as she knew it would not advance her career or vision. She instead invested all her time and energy in Global Deaf Women.

"You don't have to know everything or have all the ingredients," says Sofia. "It's important to have a clear vision, and the resources and people will show up at the right time and place." She believes in practicing patience when things aren't working out, for everything has its own purpose for us to learn from and use in our journeys. In her journey over the last several years, Sofia has proudly hosted annual "Power of Me" retreats. There, Deaf women have the opportunity to meet Deaf motivational speakers and network with other Deaf women, and they are inspired to recharge their lives and businesses. Currently, Sofia is living her dream by traveling the world with her family and taking Global Deaf Women to the next level with a refreshed mind and vision.

**"Trust your flow; it is the Light of your life. When doubt or fear shows up, it is a sign to shift your way of thinking so your inner Light keeps flowing."**

# Virginia Shou
## *Graphic Designer and Urban Farmer*

In an urban jungle like New York City, green spaces are hidden treasures. They don't just magically exist, though--people like Virginia Shou work to cultivate these spaces. A graphic designer by trade, Virginia soon found herself in Los Angeles, a city dominated by entertainment. Her work there focused on logos, branding identity, and print design, and she had a steady stream of clients--but she still had plenty of free time.

One day, a friend related how she worked for a farm-to-table restaurant in downtown Los Angeles. The farm was looking for volunteers to work in Venice, two miles from where Virginia lived. When she pulled up to the farm, she was blown away. The farm was actually on someone's front lawn. It was packed with seven raised beds full of leafy greens, lemongrass, sorrel, and turnips, and there were Spanish malbars and other vines growing on the gates. As soon as she walked through the gates, she was put right to work weeding.

If you ask the average person whether they enjoy weeding, their answer will be most likely be an emphatic no. But for Virginia, weeding ended up being quite therapeutic. The more she went back, the more her love for gardening grew. Gardening was a great excuse to get away from her computer. It enabled her to turn off chaotic, creative, and repetitive thoughts, and it helped her focus on simple tasks.

"Gardening soothes my mind and makes my soul sing. We tend to the vegetables with positive and happy vibes, and they grow back with unconditional love," Virginia says.

She decided to move back across the country to New York City, continuing her career as a graphic designer and moving her design studio to Brooklyn. Along with her design projects, Virginia is creating potential urban farming projects in the city. To nourish her farming fix, she volunteers at community gardens in New York, and still lends her hand on farms whenever she visits Los Angeles. Her dream is to expand her business in New York, running a culinary farm-to-table program and hosting workshops.

**"Once you find your passion, try and run with it. Work shouldn't feel like work; it should feel like play."**

# Mary Simmons

## *Expressions Art Bar*

In Southborough, Massachusetts, there is a space where people can take a break from the chaos of this world and escape their stress. They can enjoy socializing with friends, discover their inner artists, and walk away feeling great. This fun space is a paint and sip studio, and it's perfect for owner Mary Simmons not only as a business, but a creative outlet as well.

She always wanted to pursue something in the arts as in education. As an art teacher, she'd worked at a Deaf school for over a decade when she went back to school herself to obtain her Certificate of Advanced Graduate Study in educational leadership with a focus in the arts. While she was studying possible options for leadership, Mary started exploring the paint and sip business and hosting paint parties on the side.

She finished her degree while teaching K-12 full time, running a painting party business, and raising two children at the same time. "I was pumping milk between classes in a dirty art closet at work with excruciating pain, thinking to myself that something needed to change," she says. "Instead of breaking down, I decided to hit the pause button." She and her husband ventured off to Hawaii for their fifth anniversary, and it transformed everything for her.

"When we returned, I handed in a letter of resignation and pursued the paint and sip business full time," says Mary. "I do wish I had taken courses before diving in and learning on the job." But Mary is no stranger to problem-solving. Her philosophy is that above all, you simply need to believe in your product and what your mission is. "Don't commit until you're ready to put in the sweat," she cautions. Her weightiest sacrifice has been the financial investments she's put in, but for her, having optimism and faith to invest in herself is Light.

**"Learn to shine a light into the eyes of doubting fear. Once you realize that fear is not scary and doubts are lies, you can do anything."**

# Julie Rems Smario

## Activist and Founder of DeafHope

Julie Rems Smario considers her own heart a powerful force to be reckoned with. "Whenever my heart sparks, I follow that spark," she attests. "Whenever I see something that's not right, it becomes my mission to make it right for our humanity." Julie has spent her life fighting for what she believes is right. In 2003, the spark inside her led her to a group of people with a shared vision for what would become DeafHope, a Deaf survivor-centered agency to end domestic and sexual violence. Julie served as the founding executive director of DeafHope for eight years.

In 2010, she drove out to Sacramento to join the Deaf community in protest of a communications bill California was trying to pass at the time. This fueled her passion for advocacy in the area of Deaf children's language acquisition rights regarding American Sign Language and English, and she joined the group LEAD-K as their Public Relations Director to fight for this. For Julie, language is Light because it gives you the ability to connect with and love yourself and others, and with love, there is Light. Julie realized after taking Deaf Studies courses that she did not receive full access to language growing up. Since taking those classes, it has been her goal to prevent other Deaf children from going through the same experience. "Deaf people must be in the driver's seat to create educational laws and policies," she says.

Going to college, she was floored when she encountered many Deaf women role models who had a powerful influence on her leadership style. Despite this, she wishes she had known to trust her highly intuitive instincts. She did not trust herself enough during her younger days, dismissing her talent as an empath. Now that she is in her 50s, Julie has learned to nurture her gifts after many episodes of beratingherself for not listening to her inner "voice." She believes it is more important than anything else to be open to constructive feedback. "It's actually nourishment for personal and professional growth," says Julie. "You don't grow from positive input alone."

**"That Light you are born with, follow it. Do not let it go dark with other people's lack of faith."**

# Marilyn Jean Smith

## Consultant, Founder of Abused Deaf Women's Advocacy Services

Her deep commitment to social activism is what ignited a fire in Marilyn Jean Smith and prompted her journey into business as the founder of ADWAS, Abused Deaf Women's Advocacy Services. She wanted to set up an agency that provided services to Deaf victims of violence, frustrated by the way she'd been treated in the aftermath of her rape experience with no resources available at the time. Blazing with passion, Marilyn quit her job to put all her energy into helping other Deaf survivors. ADWAS was founded in 1986 in the basement of her home with 20 volunteers and $4,000 in startup funds, and when Marilyn retired in 2011, the agency had its own building and a budget exceeding one million dollars.

However, in the early years of her fight for services for abused Deaf women, the work ADWAS was doing wasn't seen as important. "There was resentment that our organization even existed," she says. But she persisted, eventually building an 8.6-million-dollar capital campaign for a transitional housing project called "A Place of Our Own," which is one of her proudest accomplishments. Over the years, ADWAS has played a large role in transforming how sexual and domestic violence is viewed in the Deaf community, and Marilyn has been at the forefront. She is now considered the "Mother" of the anti-violence movement in Deaf America.

Marilyn notes that it's absolutely crucial to have both a strong sense of integrity and a genuine love for humanity in order to run a business. "The ability to apologize for your own wrongdoings is essential, as well as a willingness to learn from mistakes," she says. In fact, she encourages young Deaf girls to welcome mistakes, strengthening their resilience "muscle" so that they can better endure the storms of life. "Dreams might change over time, and that's okay," Marilyn reassures. "You'll get to the one that's 'it.'"

At 67, she recognizes that she herself is still a work in progress. "I actively work on how I can better contribute to healing the ills of this world," says Marilyn. Since its founding, the ADWAS model has been replicated all over the United States, mostly in programs trained by ADWAS through a federally-funded project called "Justice for All Deaf Victims National Training." Marilyn has received an honorary Doctor of Laws degree from Gallaudet University, and has been recognized with both the Ford Foundation's Leadership for a Changing World award and a special award from President Clinton. With beautiful fortitude, she has taken her personal trauma and reshaped it into something she believes in wholeheartedly, empowering the Deaf community to prevent the same trauma from happening to others.

**"Light for me has primarily meant two things: the fire inside of me that was born out of anger and that kept my passion alive for so many years, and the many awakenings I experienced over time--both large and small--that fed my soul and therefore my growth as a human."**

# Storm Smith

## *Art Director and Filmmaker*

Storm Smith has known her inner gifts as a true artist since the age of five, always seeking to shine a different perspective on ordinary things in life. Her first love was drawing, but be it painting, writing, acting, dancing, filming, or directing, Storm is always reaching for the next big thing in her art. She is a natural storyteller and always incorporates storytelling in her creative work, which has become her niche.

While in the midst of making decisions for college, Storm was shut down by her vocational rehabilitation counselor when she said she wanted to major in theater and film. She was pressured to shift her direction to psychology, where she planned to pursue a career in counseling and therapy. This all changed when she created and submitted her first short film to the World Deaf Cinema Festival. It was at that moment that her passion was fiercely reawakened--she saw the true focus on the process of creativity, how an idea formed into reality. "I felt it, I saw it, and I experienced it. It was a natural high for me," says Storm.

But it was advice from the theatre chair at Gallaudet University that really struck a chord with Storm. "He told me I could either play it safe as a school counselor," she says, "or take a risk and pursue the career of my dreams and be much happier." That was it--she made the difficult call to resign from the counseling program at Gallaudet University to pursue her career in visual media, communications, film, and marketing. In 2016, her passions led her to work for President Bobbi Cordano, the first Deaf woman president of Gallaudet University. Cordano saw something in her and and created the position of Creative Producer, in which Storm led the efforts that saw Cordano become the most visually documented president in Gallaudet's history. Storm's work then caught the eye of BBDO Worldwide, one of the top ten advertising agencies in the world.

She is the only Black Deaf woman working as an art director at BBDO with 15,000 employees. Her long-term goal is to become a creative director and dive into visual storytelling. For Storm, it was powerful to learn that it is okay not to know everything and not to decide everything all at once. "Take time to know who you are wholeheartedly and work on yourself as you are your own craft," says Storm.

**"Be in your element. When you are in your element, you'll feel anything is possible. When you feel that, ride on it and manifest anything you want."**

PROD. Nº

DIRECTOR

CAMERA

ROLL

SCENE

TAKE

SOUND

# Terry Smith-Rawecki

## Gosia's Pierogies

Terry Smith-Rawecki has been fortunate to grow up with all the business mentors she could ever need. Any knowledge she needed, she could ask her family members--running a business runs in her family. Initially from Eastern Europe, Terry absolutely loved making pierogies. "It was a hobby, but I had so much fun I decided to make it a business," she says.

She and her husband dove in together, making all the pierogies in their own kitchen. Soon after, her sister-in-law flew in from Poland to join the business, and then from there they expanded. Terry obtained a food health certificate to sell through suppliers, added more food options to her repertoire for festivals, and now sells over 10,000 dozens of pierogies every summer month. "We're hardworking, family-oriented, and focused on providing the best possible food," she says. Her pierogies have even won a Best Tasting Pierogies award.

Like many self-made business owners, at some point she found herself at a crossroads, needing to make a decision. Should she continue working at her day job as a teacher and spend the little time leftover doing everything she can to foster her business, or should she quit her stable job in favor of channelling 100% of her energy into the success of her business? Leaving her position as a teacher was one of the most challenging decisions she had to make, but she loves having her own schedule and interacting with her customers.

Stability is only one of the things she has had to sacrifice. "I'm there all the time, working overnight to make sure everything's running smoothly," says Terry. "I have to make sure everything works out. Customers come first." She describes the enormous patience and persistence necessary in the beginning stages of starting up a business. "Stay focused and stay on track," she advises. "Don't be afraid to try. You will succeed."

No matter what challenges she is facing--whether she needs to hire more workers, if she should have three different shifts for her business, if she should run more food overnight--Terry strives to work as hard as she can. "Value yourself and stay within your goals," she says. "You'll overcome your challenges." She stresses the importance of not taking anything personally, as people have different tastes. She simply moves on and keeps going, as with every other challenge in her business.

**"Be yourself, that's where your Light is."**

"Only you can create the healthy balance
you need to fully participate
in this thing called Life."

Marilyn J. Smith

# Maria Solovey

## Maria Solovey Collection

When her parents walked in on three-year-old Maria Solovey playing with a sewing needle, there was a moment of shock as they realized she knew exactly what she was doing with it. "I knew how to use it; they trusted me," she laughs. "From my imagination, I was able to create clothes for my dolls, and I never stopped sewing."

Maria was born and raised in Ukraine and immigrated to the United States at 12 years old. She came with a dream of owning her own business as a fashion designer, and she spent all of her high school years working to achieve her dream. If it had anything to do with fashion, Maria was handling it. "I sewed clothes, hosted fashion runways, and I even used to negotiate with David's Bridal in order to let me borrow their dresses for shows," she says. She graduated as valedictorian with an acceptance letter from the Art Institute of New York, but life interfered and she ended up not attending.

It wasn't until Global Deaf Women's business competition that she finally launched her company. After having her daughter, Princess Lola Tanchik-Solovey, she wanted to dress her in a timeless style but found that none of the children's stores carried much other than bright pink and low-quality frills for girls. That was when she started designing classic, high-quality clothing in neutral colors for her daughter. When she won Global Deaf Women's competition, she opened up her business and started selling her clothes online.

Maria feels it's important to start small in order to minimize the risk of ending up indebted to a bank or another person. "It's not easy and it requires a lot of patience, but I found ways to make it grow from my own pocket," she says. She advises young Deaf girls to do the same, because consistency and patience will ultimately work out in your favor. Her family is her biggest support system, especially her brother, with whom she works. "If it's not my day, my brother will always push to remind me of the positive things," she says.

**"If you need Light to come into your life, you have to stand where it is shining."**

# Melody Stein

## *Mozzeria*

Located in the vibrant Mission District of San Francisco, known for its ever-changing regulations and laws, one business fights to be creative while staying in survival mode. Mozzeria, a Deaf-owned and -operated pizzeria, has been recognized and revered by *The New York Times*, *The Washington Post*, and *San Francisco Chronicle* for its unique and innovative pizzas. The woman behind the brilliance is Melody Stein, who runs this nationally-acclaimed pizzeria with a team of all Deaf employees.

As a child she had always dreamed of starting up a business from scratch, but she waited and waited for the right time. "I started to realize there is no such thing as the 'right time' unless you make it happen," she says. "That was when I became determined to launch Mozzeria." She previously thought that working in different fields to gain experience and saving money would put her in a better position to open a business, but she soon realized it was irrelevant. "I sort of wish I had opened the restaurant years ago," she confesses. "I've seen twentysomethings start successful businesses."

One of their biggest challenges is communicating with their hearing patrons and educating business owners around them on how to work with the Deaf community. It's part of figuring out how to stay one step ahead, according to Melody. Whenever they struck hardship in the process of building their business, support would flood in from online. "I'd have moments of self-doubt, and supporters who read Mozzeria's blog would tell me not to give up, that they were rooting for me," she recalls. "I would look to my family and friends for support and they helped guide me through realizing my dreams."

Drive, determination, and passion are what she credits as the keys to success; however, the credit for Mozzeria's sumptuous pizza goes to the special 5,000-pound Stefano Ferrara oven from Italy they use. They've been able to flourish and earn genuine rave reviews from customers all over the world despite the challenge of operating their business in San Francisco, one of the most expensive cities in the nation. Mozzeria has also been voted one of San Francisco's 50 Best Restaurants and made the list of Yelp's 100 Most Popular Restaurants, which Melody considers to be some of her proudest feats in addition to, of course, launching Mozzeria.

**"You are in charge of your life, don't let anyone else tell you what to do with it. Be you."**

# Rosetta "Zetta" Stevenson

## *Zetta Marie's Patisserie*

Growing up, wanting to be a teacher was the popular career goal at the time, and she was no different than her peers. However, when she opened a can of grape juice at age four, she knew at that moment that her future would be in the kitchen--she just wasn't sure how. She soon fell in love with baking after her grandmother asked her to bake with her. "We'd make apple pies, pecan pies, sweet potato pies," she says.

She would try baking at home, much to her mother's chagrin. "My mom was afraid I wouldn't be able to hear when I baked," Rosetta says. She continued taking home economics classes at school in order to continue baking away from home.

"When I graduated, my mom asked me what I wanted to do," Rosetta says, explaining she couldn't sit there and do nothing. She'd known since four years old that she was made to be in the kitchen. "I told her I wanted to cook, to bake--and she encouraged me to look up cooking schools," says Rosetta.

She fought to find her way into the food industry, but it was difficult to find anyone willing to hire a Deaf individual. "I was told to start my own business," she says. "I didn't let all the frustrations and challenges stop me." During her low points, she would often look to her mother, a single parent of three, for inspiration. "My mom and grandmother really helped motivate me; I didn't need a man to lift me up," says Rosetta.

Rosetta opened a brick-and-mortar bakery, ZettaMarie's Patisserie, after searching for the right location for months in Colorado. Her favorite delicacies are European pastries using international spices. Today, she has been running her business for five years and has stacked up three degrees. It is her hope that young Deaf girls will dream big in the pursuit of their aspirations. "Don't give up; find support," she encourages. "If you can't find it in others, find it in yourself."

**"Shining your Light means showing the world what you have. Show them your talents, your skills, show them what you are good at."**

# Gina Swanson

## Swanson's Holistic Hands

Gina Swanson's vision for the world is full of Light. As a holistic lifestyle coach, she works with people to clarify their energy in the midst of a chaotic life. With her guidance, clients uncover and confront their trauma using natural healing remedies and tools such as tarot cards, crystal energy, essential oils, and reiki healing. Gina educates her clients on the vital process of spiritual care so they may use their inner Light to work toward a healthier mind, body, and spirit.

Growing up, she always wanted to work in health and be a nurse. She remembers her grandmother fondly, how she saved a newborn's life with virtually no training. Gina followed in her footsteps, but soon found she didn't like needles and traded in her dream of becoming a nurse. However, as a DeafBlind woman diagnosed with fibromyalgia, she was unable to work outside her home. Gina first ventured into making and selling soy candles, but after fighting to try and prove herself, she received no support from her vocational rehabilitation counselor. She continued working, but she knew the drive to create her own business would not be quelled.

One day, her husband took her hands and demonstrated how she can use energy to connect with a higher force, the flickering heat over her palms awakening her spirit. She then decided to take the plunge and request funding for her business plan to set up private holistic health courses in her area. After her request for funding was approved, she began networking as a holistic health practitioner and obtained over 20 certifications. She then evolved into a holistic lifestyle coach and now also presents motivational speeches on incorporating a wholly fulfilling lifestyle like hers. Her greatest challenge? Being onstage and unable to see the audience's facial expressions, their a-ha! moments that she cherishes seeing in her coaching clients.

But Gina, with her unbreakable spirit and fierce belief in her own dreams, considers herself living proof that there are no barriers to keep you from accomplishing your dreams. When asked what she wishes she knew before she started, Gina's simple reply is that there is nothing to wish, everything is in the Divine Plan. She trusts her intuition, her Light, and has faith in her lifestyle of choice to bring joy to herself and others.

**"The Light is like when you first make eye contact with someone you fall in love with."**

# Maureen Sydnor

## *Aqua Bliss*

Growing up, Maureen Sydnor moved with her family all around the United States because her father was in the Air Force. No one ever asked her what she wanted to be when she grew up; she simply did whatever her parents did, like water skiing, ice skating, traveling, and hiking. She was particularly passionate about swimming and eagerly got her first job as a lifeguard and water safety instructor, teaching kids how to swim. Shortly after, she studied physical education at her university and was even on the diving team one year.

For years she found herself swept up in her work as a senior loan closer for the mortgage industry before attempting her dream. Maureen had never really thought about the future, she confesses--but at 55 years old, she began envisioning her dream of being a swimming instructor again. That's how Maureen found a job as a part-time swimming instructor, until she was told that since she couldn't hear the whistle, it wasn't safe when a child was struggling in the water. She was absolutely crushed and slid into a state of depression.

Everything changed one day when a new facility opened up nearby and she was determined to apply to work at the pool again. The interviewer asked if she would be able to teach yoga in the water, and instantly her intuition told her to say "Yes, I can!" With encouragement from Sofia Seitchik with Global Deaf Women, she opened her own business. From that moment on, she saw herself as an Aqua Whisperer. She now leads senior citizens and the physically challenged to discover joy in water movement and also helps them achieve strengths and emit positive energy through Aqua Kriya Yoga and Ai Chi in the aquatic therapy.

"I teach my students to discover joy, healing, and love through uplifting vibrational energy and soul-soothing water techniques," Maureen says. It was difficult for her to get interpreters, but after three years she finally got her certificates in Ai Chi and Aqua Kriya Yoga. However, she now realizes she didn't need that validation. It's not about doing it by the book--it's about using your gifts. Now aiming to build a thermal pool for her business, she encourages Deaf girls to go with the flow when they start their own businesses. "Making mistakes will produce great results in the end," she promises.

**"Shining my Light means to me that you have to follow your heart to the Light of what makes you happy in life, and then open your heart to the world."**

# Jennifer Tandoc

## Jennifer Tandoc Art and Photography

Passion is the key to one's future, according to Jennifer Tandoc, a Deaf artist and photographer originally from the Philippines. "It's important to have passion so that you can be persistent in running your business," she says. "It guarantees your skills will improve." One way of identifying where your passion lies is by listening to people when they tell you what you're good at. That's how Jennifer realized she wanted to become an artist in her formative years at school. She moved to America at two years old and found it easy to live in a different culture, citing her experience at California School for the Deaf, Riverside as one of the best in her life. "It helped me become who I am," says Jennifer. "People really liked my drawings; I was told that I had talent. From there I knew I wanted to be an artist."

She initially worked different jobs that had little relevance to art, such as working full-time for her state's government. "When I moved to Austin, I saw so many different types of art everywhere," she marvels. "It inspired me to start taking my artwork seriously and start up my art business." Shortly after, she left her job with the government and began finding more time to work on her art on a daily basis. She now runs her own business, Jennifer Tandoc Art and Photography, where she provides freelance photography work for special occasions and utilizes different art mediums such as zentangle or technical black ink to create spatial artwork.

"It's never too late to get started, but I do wish I had started earlier--that someone would have encouraged me to start earlier," she says. "But it was me who needed to decide that I needed to start my business." At the outset, it was difficult for her to recognize her own value in her unique art, but social media and being able to see people's reactions to her art online has helped build her confidence. "I've been surrounded by positivity, which helps me express myself better."

She has been recognized by Convo, The Daily Moth, and Insight Via Traveling Eyes for her artistic contributions. Jennifer is constantly coming up with new ideas and designs and scrambling to create them before her mind fades or distorts them. In pursuing her dream, she had to surrender the stable government job she had with all its benefits and financial security. But as she advises young Deaf women, it's so important to stay focused on your business. "Don't waste your skill; don't hide your talents," she urges. "Show the world your art."

**"Keep finding your passion by going through various experiences in life. Without your passion, you can't succeed."**

# Melinni "Mel" Taylor

## Deaf Future Works

When Melinni "Mel" Taylor was younger, she had dreams of becoming Wonder Woman. That was her role model, because she loved how she embodied strength in a powerful woman. By way of becoming a benefits counselor, she has turned into a Wonder Woman of sorts for the Deaf community in Austin, Texas. Mel helps Deaf individuals determine how to maximize their benefits through SSI, SSDI, Medicare, Medicaid, and all other programs provided to them by the government.

Originally, Mel worked as a mental health counselor for many years until she realized one day she was simply burnt out--so she stayed at home raising the kids. But when the kids would go back to school full-time after summer break, she would quickly grow bored. She sought services from Vocational Rehabilitation to figure out her next career step, and after a few assessments was told social work was the best fit due to her background.

"I felt mental health counseling wasn't a good fit for me personally," she explains. "But there was a great need for benefits counselors through the Department of Rehabilitation Services, so I trained and got my certifications." Mel had anxiety about trying to start her own business, compounded by a fear of failure. This stemmed from her childhood, when she was sent off to live with her teacher at four years old. As a result, Mel struggled with the feeling that she was not valued and wanted, and a fear of rejection--but decided to confront her fears head on.

Mel took the plunge and set up her own business. She has learned to embrace fear, rather than run away from it. There's nowhere else to go but forward. "Business improves ourselves and what we know," she says. "I wouldn't be able to learn as much about myself with a 9-to-5 job."

She loves passing on her Light to others, especially seeing when her clients' eyes light up when they understand something for the first time. Mel loves putting people at ease so they can feel confident about returning to work--she consider her Light to be the moment when other people understand and accomplish their own purposes.

**"I know we all have Light inside of us that radiates energy for others to see...you need to find that Light, what motivates you, and feed it."**

# Dr. Angela K. Trahan

## *Deaf Global Solutions*

Dr. Angela Trahan has a knack for navigating the delicate intersection of parent choice and Deaf expertise when it comes to hearing parents making decisions for their deaf and hard of hearing children. As Dr. Trahan is well aware, this issue can be a source of tension in the community. She was almost fired twice as an educator for advising parents on their children's Individualized Education Plans, or IEPs. But in her many years of work in K-12 Deaf education, she was increasingly shocked by the lack of resources and disparity in education for Deaf children.

Having gone through the trials and tribulations that come with being a deaf child herself, she watched her hearing mom fighting for the right IEP that would provide her with the most accessible education. Now with a Master's degree, a Doctorate in Deaf Education, and a decade's worth of experience in teaching K-12 Deaf education under her belt, Dr. Angela K. Trahan has come to find a passion for collaborating with parents to act in the best interest of each child. After leaving her post as an educator, she moved in the direction she felt called and launched Deaf Global Solutions, which seeks to establish a high-achieving team of people with the Deaf Gain awareness. They also provide professional development and advocacy training to parents with deaf and hard of hearing children all over the world. Dr. Trahan has become a guide and mentor for parents who want to ensure their children's success.

In 2016 she began writing a dissertation on parents' experiences with IEPs and their deaf children, and she was often lit with rage and brought to tears throughout the process of studying how America's lack of accommodations and quality Deaf education affects deaf students nationally. However, Dr. Trahan says this only contributed to her stubbornness in finishing her dissertation, which she has presented at several conferences and plans to continue doing so.

Finding a healthy balance between her personal and business commitments has proven to be the most difficult part of running her business. Dr. Trahan, who has no degree in business administration, says hiring a business coach was also vital to the process. She encourages all young Deaf girls to be present with themselves while the manifestation of their dreams is taking place. She is currently working on manifesting her dream of connecting the entire Deaf population in the the Greater Houston area by securing a facility to create a community center for local Deaf residents.

**"Choose your mentor to encourage you to reach toward your dreams!"**

# Anna Virnig
## *Rawland Cycles*

Anna Virnig and her husband Sean started up Rawland in Northfield, Minnesota when they noticed how bicycles should handle on dirt and gravel in the country where there is almost always stiff crosswind. Being Deaf, they were concerned with the unique challenges they faced. Sean avoided cars and trucks traveling at high speed from behind by riding on the shoulder of roads that are usually covered in loose dirt and gravel. This was what led to development of the design platform for which Rawland is well known; Rawland is essentially the ferrous personification of Deaf Gain. When they presented their idea to several reputable custom bike builders, they were told their idea was far too radical and it couldn't be done. That was the turning point for them--they simply took it upon themselves.

For ten years and counting, Rawland Cycles has designed and produced quality bicycles with custom features. The vision has always been to cater to discerning cyclists who relish traditional yet modern takes on high-end adventure touring bicycles. They started up Rawland at a time when design challenges for bicycling out in the country with an endlessly beating wind were not fully understood nor addressed by the cycling industry then.

With both Anna and Sean at the helm, Rawland has since garnered at least six Best of Show awards for their design and products at the world's biggest and most competitive industry trade show for bicycles. Rawland has also been featured in numerous mainstream magazines such as Outside and Men's Journal.

"The process has been blood, sweat, and tears at every stroke of the pedal," Anna says. "But I've learned to embrace and appreciate this, especially as a Deaf woman." She describes how when she was younger, doctors discouraged her parents from using American Sign Language with her, and it wasn't until her first day in a Deaf program that she really thrived. "This set me on the right path," she says, "and definitely changed my life for the better."

The unyielding faith Anna has in herself and her devotion to her company's mission is what keeps her going. It is essential to Anna to maintain such conviction in what Rawland does for her business and life, and to be inspired and convinced by what Rawland brings to the market and the role it has in both the industry and its customers and their experiences. Those two key traits resonate with everything else Anna does as the Deaf woman in a competitive, ever-changing industry. Anna is continually inspired to be a woman of class with a perpetual smile on her face, because she knows there are no failures--only lessons.

**"Shining the Light within you is like the North Star. Be conscious, for sharing the Light will navigate you and others through life."**

# Elise "Lisi" Whitworth

## Eventida

After many experiences attending events that end up disappointing her with their lack of accessibility and information, frustration got the better of Elise "Lisi" Whitworth. "My motivation is personal," she explains. "As someone who loves attending seminars and workshops, I want it to be easy and painless to request an ASL interpreter and soy-free meals, as I have an allergy." Ever since she was 25 years old, Lisi knew she wanted to run an events business. She got started by becoming a certified event planner and building her first website, EyeonEvents.com, but someone ended up seeing it and asking her to do their website as well. "Before I knew it, I was doing web development full-time and had managed over 300 projects," Lisi says.

For many years, the initial vision for her website, now called Eventida, evolved while Lisi and her husband and partner, Lee, ran a creative services firm dedicated to helping clients grow their audience through websites, events, and Internet marketing. As they served clients, they slowly built Eventida into an events bulletin board and marketplace, making more inclusive events accessible and transforming Eventida into a global brand. At heart, it is everyday consumers going online to find or promote accommodations for their events. Most of all, it is about building relationships with others who share the same philosophy of inclusion.

"Once I truly embraced the real me, I started to feel the Light in me once again burn as strongly as it used to," says Lisi. Her journey to becoming the woman she is today isn't comprised of merely one story, but instead is like a tapestry weaved with stories from all of her experiences with childhood, marriage, entrepreneurship, motherhood, illness, and multiple brushes with death.

She admits it's tempting to wonder what might have been if they had taken the leap sooner with Eventida, but acknowledges the experience she gained through her journey has been imperative to getting to where she is now. When she needs a boost of confidence, she reminds herself of every client of hers that became a success story and the fact that she had managed to run the business while dealing with multiple illnesses, including cancer and six months of brutal chemotherapy.

Lisi was recognized in 2014 as one of the 30 Women to Watch by Utah Business. She acknowledges her success as a result of her constant drive to learn and likens herself to a sponge, soaking up everything to acquire new knowledge, develop new skills, and hone her existing ones. Her advice to other Deaf women: "With patience, persistence, and learning—success will come."

**"To me, sharing my Light means sharing all the passion and ideas I have, not hoarding them. While 'shining your Light' means letting yourself shine proudly, don't hide yourself or try and turn the light on someone else."**

# Wendy Wiatrowski
## *Savvy Assistants*

As a child, Wendy Wiatrowski and her sister spent their days playing "Library," creating sign-out cards inside of books and materials to check out. From a young age, she was enthralled with the idea of working in an office environment and was happy running errands for others. "I've always enjoyed tasks that required efficiency and detail, so it was a natural transition after graduating from Gallaudet to work in an organizational management-oriented position at the same institution," Wendy says.

Even though she loved her job, the 9-to-5 hustle began to stress her out. She was tired of the commute and tired of running her life by the clock. Wendy longed for the freedom of working for herself so she explored some options, including owning a consignment store. A visit to a local store made her realize she wanted to run a virtual company from the comfort of her home—and Savvy Assistants was born. She was doing what she truly loved to do: running errands, handling details, and paperwork—only this time it was on her own terms, making the work so much more satisfying.

Wendy credits the support of her husband, friends, mentors, and colleagues for helping her get through challenges and moments of doubt. The usual cliché still works: life is short. Have a passion for what you want to do and go for it, because every challenge has a solution, according to Wendy.

"I wish I had known I could do this earlier in life. I was simply doing what society expected me to do—doing my part in bringing home the bacon, doing what I could to ensure gender equality in the workplace, and so on," Wendy says. "But then I realized it's not about that—it's about me, taking care of myself, and doing what I want. Changing my mindset has allowed me to be the happiest I've ever been."

It is this positive mindset that Wendy wants to share with others, especially young Deaf girls. "If you have a passion, do it as early as you can or want," Wendy says. "Don't let anything hold you back." For Wendy, Light means your "inner drive," the passion coming from your heart and soul that's helping you move forward, making a difference in the world and communicating from your soul in your own unique way.

**"You can choose to accept your life as it is or do something about it.  Even one step forward will spark a change in your life."**

# Dorothy "Narayani" Wilkins
## Deaf Roots and Wings

The best part about Dorothy "Narayani" Wilkins' job is seeing the smiles on her students' faces as they take the time to pamper themselves with yoga and their stress melts away. She herself sacrifices much of her time between the various services she provides and the pursuit of her dream to work with Deaf people from all walks of life to embrace a healthy lifestyle via yoga and holistic approaches to raise positive energy and promote being present in life.

Dorothy was teaching classes at NTID when they denied her tenure in 1999. Reeling from the disappointment, she started taking training courses in order to become a Reiki practitioner. She was already teaching yoga classes on the side, so she decided to expand it into a full-blown business--and Deaf Roots and Wings was born. As Dorothy says, "Wings show you what you can become. Roots remind you where you're from." She gave workshops at Deaf Women United conferences around the nation and also worked with the DeafYoga Foundation.

It was through this foundation that she embarked on a month-long teacher training course at a yoga ranch in 2010, which she considers the first major turning point in her life. There, she was given her spiritual name, "Narayani," and soon after started training to be a life coach in addition to running her yoga business. She then found a co-host in Deborah Mayer and they began hosting Deaf Yoga and Life retreats, sometimes traveling across several states to present.

"Om, I shine when I teach!" she smiles. "Om, I always enjoyed learning and teaching about life...it is never too late. Om, I am only 60 years old." At one point, the struggle to balance her day job as an ASL professor with teaching yoga, traveling for Deaf Yoga and Life retreats, and doing coaching sessions on the side became especially difficult. In the midst of trying to balance all of this, she learned that her mother had Alzheimer's disease, and she took care of her until the very end. As for her own support system, she has her husband, business coach, good friends, and her business partner to help her through her lowest moments of self-doubt. Dorothy is so grateful to have found the Universe and a form of recovery through yoga, having battled alcoholism and food addiction. "The Light, to me and my business, is the simpatico relationship I have with myself and with others on a soul level," she says of Deaf Roots and Wings.

**"Go forward and pursue your dream--fight the barriers and challenges you face and have the noblest hunger to conquer all!"**

# Melissa Elmira Yingst

## News Anchor and Activist

Melissa Elmira Yingst is an incredibly genuine person, which can be a difficult trait to find working in television. As a child, she looked up to Deaf anchors Gil Eastman and Mary Lou Novitsky on Deaf Mosaic and decided she wanted to be a reporter. From reading her grandma's gossip magazines and writing up her own reviews, to working with *What's Up Gallaudet* at her alma mater, Gallaudet University, to landing a job after graduation with the Deaf and Hearing Network (DHN) in Arizona, Melissa is a reporter through and through.

Melissa is a huge advocate for both the Latinx and the Deaf communities, using her experiences as a Deaf Latina woman to spread awareness and help women overcome societal expectations. She finds that being true to her Latina heritage and discovering her roots helps her be genuine in her reporting--by showing that she is a real person just like her viewers.

She's always loved writing stories, finding a vulnerability in the openness that allowed her to relate to other people. However, it wasn't until she got the job with DHN that she got her first real opportunity to craft stories and learn how to discuss them, her favorite being a LEAD-K issue. Her work with DHN won her a 2015 Gracie Award for Anchor of the Year, from the Alliance for Women in Media.

Melissa remembers what it felt like investing so much time and energy into DHN, and the devastating heartbreak when their funding ran out. She then transitioned to DPAN TV, where she does investigative reporting in order to bring light to issues faced by the Deaf community and beyond, often reporting on world news as well. She feels that working with a team like DPAN TV offers great support, giving her a better chance to grow and contribute than does working alone. "And of course, you can never underestimate the power of red lipstick," she jokes.

"Shining my Light means owning it, being real," Melissa says. She believes in developing connections and having genuine relationships with other people, which requires authenticity--something she weaves into everything she does, particularly on camera. "Sometimes I'll receive heavy criticism when I'm reporting, but I see criticism as an opportunity to grow," she says, preferring to view it with a positive attitude. "Everything has a purpose."

**"We can't always predict the future, but I know I'll always have opportunities come my way."**

175

# Shiran Zhavian

## *Stem Cell Lab Technologist*

As a child at Lexington School for the Deaf, Shiran Zhavian was excited and motivated by every minute she spent in a math class. "I found solving problems fun and therapeutic," she says. Teachers predicted that she would become a math teacher, but later in high school she discovered her real passion--chemistry, where she always felt a fire of excitement burning.

Born in Israel, Shiran is a Persian-Israeli who moved to New York City when she was seven years old. Her journey was at times difficult, experiencing the deaths of both of her parents in her childhood--first her father when she was just three years old, and later her mother when she was ten. Her adoptive mother, Adele, fell in love with Shiran's big, curious eyes and strong personality--and before her death, she promised Shiran's mother that she would be loved and lead a successful life. Indeed, Shiran has broken barriers in areas where Persian women are traditionally oppressed, finding success in the science field.

After obtaining her master's degree, Shiran worked in a Deaf school for two years, teaching science courses to high school students. Feeling an urge to solve the world's problems as a chemist, Shiran began researching other opportunities that would allow her to put her skills to the test. She attended a career fair for scientists with disabilities and landed what she calls her dream job.

Shiran now works for the New York Blood Center, where she is immersed in the hearing world. Through her work, she processes stem cells from patients and cryo-preserves the cells until it is time for infusion and the cells are sent back to them, creating new healthy blood cells. Shiran describes working in this environment as a kind of sacrifice, leaving the Deaf community behind for a more isolating job in pursuit of her passion.

"I take my dreams very seriously," she says. "I always thought about getting out of my comfort zone and making a difference in the world as a scientist." In spreading her love of optimism, she encourages young Deaf girls to run after their dreams with full enthusiasm. "Go to camps, go to events, go to summer programs," she suggests. "Ask people for advice and find role models. Basically, get as much experience as you possibly can in your chosen field."

**"Doing what you love lights up your soul and brings beauty that shines on the world around you."**

# Heidi Zimmer

## *Mountaineer*

When Heidi was a little girl, her family lived in an old house that was built in the 1910s in Tempe, Arizona, between a church and Arizona State University. One day when she was two years old, her mother let her out of the house to play in the yard. After a while, her mother realized she couldn't find her and panicked, as any parent would.

Her mother nearly had a heart attack when she located Heidi on the roof of the house. She called Heidi's father, who was over at the church--but he was afraid of heights. Luckily, they noticed a student from the university walking by, who helped bring Heidi down from the roof. That was the moment Heidi first became inspired to climb mountains.

In addition to being Deaf, Heidi was diagnosed late in life with Usher syndrome, a progressive loss of vision due to Retinitis Pigmentosa. When she learned that, she finally understood why her balance was always poor, but it didn't stop her from pursuing her passion for climbing. One way she gets around it is by always carrying ski poles on climbs to help with balance. Her poor balance has made the climbs even more challenging, especially with loose rocks, talus, and steep climbs without snow.

Heidi's vision is to climb all of the world's seven summits, of which she has climbed three. Since then, she has become the first Deaf woman to reach the top of Mt. Kilimanjaro and Denali, and the first Deaf person to reach the top of Mt. Elbrus. Also on track to becoming the first Deaf person to reach the highest point in all 50 American states, Heidi has just eight high points remaining. Currently, she is working on climbing Colorado's 14ers, and has climbed 45 of the 75 peaks--38 of them solo.

Once, she told an instructor of hers that her dream was to climb Mt. Everest. She asked, "What do you think? Can I do it?" For the first time in her life, Heidi had a positive response from a hearing person. She said, "Why not? You can do it. Go for it." Her instructor's simple response changed her life.

**"Take risks and be creative. Be willing to try different methods even if they are uncomfortable so that you may continue to evolve and grow."**

# LaRonda Zupp
## Turtle Heart Coaching and Retreats

As a child, LaRonda Zupp dabbled with the idea of becoming an artist like her dad, or a healer like her mom who was a nurse. But as the oldest sibling, she often found herself in the role of a teacher. LaRonda was also a creative, confident, and compassionate child who had a natural gift for making people feel valued and good about themselves and their abilities.

Her gift of uplifting others is manifested through her business, Turtle Heart Coaching and Retreats, which provides women with opportunities to heal, explore, awaken, renew and transform their lives through coaching and retreats. Why the turtle? One of her goals is to inspire you to slow down, go within and progress at your own pace -- like a turtle. LaRonda's entrepreneurial journey began with her own awakening.

Prior to starting her own business, LaRonda worked in middle management in the Bay Area, serving the diverse local deaf community.. While she enjoyed many aspects of management, the day came when she knew it was time to move on. The heaviness of the workload manifested itself onto her body and she could see that her work life in that role and environment was not healthy. It lacked the joy she needed to stay fueled and focused.

The decision to leave the security of her job came from that deep voice within, from a profound place of self-love. To leave would not be selfish, but rather an act of extreme self-care. She did not know where she would go next. All she knew was that she had gone as far as she wanted to go in that role at the time. With her family's love and support, she bid farewell and leapt bravely into the unknown.

Not long after, LaRonda discovered her wise-woman calling: to help other women slow down, listen to their inner-wisdom, learn to value and care for themselves throughout life changes, and find a sense of purpose. She no longer measures success in titles or status. She now measures success by how highly she values herself; her positive connections with others; the amount of time she gets to spend with herself, family, and friends; and how soundly she sleeps at night. As a Master Retreat and Life Coach, LaRonda sees herself as a beacon, shining a light that guides women as they navigate their way toward living more authentic, balanced, whole, and fulfilled lives.

**"Lift while you climb."**

"When you visualize,
trust the vision in your confidence,
soar high in deep faith,
uncertainty will fade away,
and your inner Light shines!"

Irina M. Normatov and Sofia Seitchik

# Photography Credits

**Clare Cassidy** (*Alice Ann Friends; Ally Balsley & Brittany Noschese; Ann Marie "Jade" Bryan; Ann Meehan; Anna Virnig; Brenna DeBartolo; Dawnena Michelle Muth; Dr. E. Lynn Jacobowitz; Elise Whitworth; Gina Pasini; Gina Swanson; Irina Normatov; Irma Azrelyant; Jacqueline Roth; Jules Dameron; Julie Rems-Smario; Karen Carlson Freitas; Kavita Pipalia, Lisa Hermatz & Lauren Maucere; Kelly Doucet Simpson; LaRonda Zupp; Lori Maynard; Malene Melander; Maleni Chaitoo; Mara Ladines; Maria Solovey; Mary Simmons; Maureen Sydnor; Melissa Malzkuhn; Melissa Yingst; Melody Stein; Michelle Lapides & Katherine Lees; Patricia Ward Costello; Patty Carter; Peggy Hlibok; Rajarajeshwari; Rebecca Moir; Rezenet Moges-Riedel; Rosemary Latin; Shiran Zhavian; Sofia Seitchik; Storm Smith; Tawny Holmes; Virginia Shou; Wendy Wiatrowski; group photos p. 33, 62, 111, and 177*)

**Lindsey Higginbotham** (*Julia Cameron Damon; Arlene Garcia; Joette Paulone; Nancy Rourke; Nick Runge; Rosetta Stevenson; Sabrina Hottle-Valencia; Heidi Zimmer*)

**Jennifer Tandoc** (*Jasmine Garcia-Freeland; Sarah Morrison; Melinni Taylor; Dr. Angela K. Trahan*)

**Tiffany Saccente** (*Michelle Banks; Sharon Duchesneau and Candace McCullough; Claudia Gordon; Leah Katz-Hernandez; group photo p. 88*)

**Cat Cassidy** (*Laural Hartman; Vicki Hurwitz; Karen Putz; Dorothy Wilkins*)

**Gabby Hopkinson** (*Melissa "echo" Greenlee; Marilyn Jean Smith*)

**Kelly Doucet Simpson** (*Clare Cassidy*)

**Jiyoung Jou** (*Crystal Eusebio*)

**Shania Corley** (*CyEra Bibbs*)

**Julien McRoberts** (*Elise Nye Holliday*)

**Karen Reynoso** (*Haydee Garcia*)

**Tamara Ocuto** (*Jennifer Tandoc*)

**Ivelisse Santiago** (*Jésica Zoé Rodríguez Meléndez*)

**Dan Canon** (*Julie Dalbom*)

**Sam Harris** (*Keri Brooks*)

**Ali Mohajedi** (*Marlee Matlin*)

**Lee Jones** (*Rochella Jones*)

**Picture People** (*Dr. Suzette Garay*)

**Catalin Baicus** (*Monique Holt*)

**Jason Neubauer** (*Terrylene Sacchetti*)

**Donna Frank** (*Terry Smith-Rawecki*)

**Sindhu Amruthur** (*Smitha Hanumantha*)

**Sheena Lyles** (*Sheena Lyles*)

# The Women at a Glance

**Iris Aranda**
Artist & Founder, Irisne Fine Art
irisne.com

**Irma Azrelyant**
Co-Founder and Chief Financial Officer
Deaf and Hard of Hearing Interpreting Services
dhisnyc.com

**Ally Balsley and Brittany Noschese**
Birth and postpartum doulas
Hand Waves Birth Services
handwavesbirth.com

**Michelle Banks**
Founder/CEO of MIANBA Productions
michelleabanks.com

**CyEra Bibbs-Taylor**
Owner, Sparkle Divas Makeup Artistry
sparkledivasmakeupartistry.com

**Keri Brooks**
Co-owner, TRUE-BIZ ASL
truebizasl.com

**Ann Marie "Jade" Bryan**
Film producer and director
Jade Films and Entertainment
jadefilm.com

**Patty Carter**
PattyCakes Mobile, LLC
pattycakesmobile.com

**Clare Cassidy**
Owner, clare cassidy photography
clarecassidyphotography.com

**Maleni Chaitoo**
Producer, Actress and Advocate
malenichaitoo.com

**Patricia Ward Costello**
Entrepreneur, Herbal Soothing
herbalsoothing.com

**Julie Dalbom**
Reproduction Justice & Women's Rights Activist
kentuckyhealthjusticenetwork.org

**Julia "Jules" Dameron**
Content Producer & Supervisor of DPAN TV
dpan.tv

**Julia Cameron Damon**
Camrose Artes Infinitae &
Julia Cameron's Magical Mystical Massage Tour
juliacamerondamon.wixsite.com/cams-massage

**Brenna DeBartolo**
Founder, Forest Souls
forestsouls.com

**Kelly Doucet-Simpson**
Photographer and Animal Portrait Painter
Kelly Simpson Photography
kellysimpsonphotography.com

**Crystal Eusebio**
Assistant Director of Student Activities
Boston University

**Jasmine Garcia Freeland**
Jewelry Artist & Entrepreneur
jasminegfreeland.com

**Karen Carlson Freitas**
Artist, Founder & Entrepreneur
Treasures From Trees

**Alice Ann "Alli" Friends**
Owner, Friends Interpreting Services, LLC
friendsinterpretingservices.com

**Dr. Suzette Garay**
International/National Motivational Speaker
Baby Signs 4 U LLC
babysigns4u.com

**Arlene Garcia**
Co-founder and President, Veditz
facebook.com/veditz

**Haydee Garcia**
Founder & Travel Guide Director
Go Haydee Tours
gohaydeetours.com

**Claudia Lorraine Gordon**
Disability Rights Advocate, Sprint Accessibility
instagram.com/cascade4ever

**Melissa "echo" Greenlee**
Entrepreneur, deaffriendly
deaffriendly.com

**Smitha Hanumantha**
Founder, designer and stylist, The Zenobias
thezenobias.com

**Laural Hartman**
Owner, Dirtybeardpress
dirtybeardpress.com

**Lisa Hermatz, Lauren Maucere &
Kavita Pipalia**
Founders and Visionaries, KODAwest
kodawest.org

**Peggy O'Gorman Hlibok**
Educator, esad.org

**Elise Nye Holliday**
Owner, Santa Fe Weaving Gallery
sfweaving.com

**Tawny Holmes**
Lawyer, Advocate, Education Policy Counsel
nad.org

**Monique Holt**
Pioneer, Artist & Actress
linkedin.com/in/monique-holt-4589b010

**Sabrina Hottle-Valenica**
Owner and Lifestyle Coach/Trainer, Simple n Fit
simplenfit.com

**Vicki Hurwitz**
Pioneer & Founder
deafwomenrochester.org/herstory

**Dr. E. Lynn Jacobowitz**
CEO, ASL STAR
facebook.com/jaco.aslstar

**Rochella Jones**
Owner, 5 Wellness, LLC
5wellness.com

**Leah Katz-Hernandez**
Public Speaker, Advocate, and
Communications Consultant
linkedin.com/in/leah-katz-hernandez-7ab20835

**Mara Ladines**
Owner and artist, By Mara, LLC
bymara.com

**Michelle Lapides & Katherine Lees**
Co-founders & co-owners
dozanü innovations
dozanu.com

**Rosemary Latin**
Owner, Cake Decorator & Artist
Rosemary's Fabulous Cakes
rosemarysfabulouscakes.webstarts.com

**Sheena Lyles**
Comedian/Actress, Queen Foreverrr
facebook.com/queenforeverrr

**Melissa Malzkuhn**
Ink & Salt LLC, Motion Light Lab
theaslapp.com

**Marlee Matlin**
Emmy and Oscar Winning Actress
marleematlinsite.com

**Lori Maynard**
Celebrate Souls, LLC
celebratesouls.com

**Dr. Candace McCullough
& Sharon Duchesneau**
Counselors and co-owners
Deaf Counseling Center
deafcounseling.com

**Ann Meehan**
Realtor
The Signing Group of Real Estate Teams LLC
signinggroup.com

**Malene Melander**
Entrepreneur & Sexologist and Love Coach
sexandlove.dk

**Rebecca Moir**
Owner and Stylist, Glam by Becca
glambybecca.net

**Sarah Morrison**
ProTactile Connects & ProTactile Connections
protactileconnects.weebly.com

**Dawnena Michelle Muth**
Owner and business consultant, Dreamgivers LLC
dawnena.rocks

**Irina Miriam Normatov**
The Wealth of Joy, LLC
facebook.com/thewealthofjoy

**Gina Pasini**
Owner, Charmeleonized Ones
aabcdefginaa.etsy.com

**Joette Paulone**
Filming PAH

**Karen Putz**
Author and Motivational Speaker
Ageless Passions
agelesspassions.com

**Rajarajeshwari**
Owner, Yoga Acharya and Teacher, Deafhood Yoga
deafhoodyoga.com

**Rezenet Moges Riedel**
University Lecturer
www.cla.csulb.edu/programs/asld

**Jesica Zoe Rodriguez Melendez**
CEO, JeZoe for a happy skin
facebook.com/jezoe3

**Jacqueline "Jackie" Roth**
Licensed Associate Real Estate Broker
Douglas Elliman Real Estate
jacquelineroth.elliman.com

**Nancy Rourke**
Artist
Nancy Rourke The Latest Expressionist Paintings
nancyrourke.com

**Nicki Runge**
Freelance Business Mentor, Actress, ASL Coach,
and Artistic Director, ImaginASL
imaginasl.wix.com/imaginasl

**Terrylene Sacchetti**
ASL poet, Visionary and Founder, Fingerly Friends
terrylene.com

**Sofia Normatov Seitchik**
Vision & Mindset Coach, Conscious Business Mentor,
and Public Speaker
Global Deaf Women
globaldeafwomen.com

**Virginia Shou**
Graphic Designer and Urban Gardener
virginiashou.com

**Mary Simmons**
Artist and Owner, Expressions Art Bar
expressionsartbar.com

**Julie Rems Smario**
Founder & Activist - DeafHope and LEAD-K
asl4deafkids.org

**Marilyn Jean Smith**
Founder and Former Executive Director
Abused Deaf Women's Advocacy Services
adwas.org

**Storm Smith**
Filmmaker & Motivational Speaker
officialstormsmith.com

**Terry Smith-Rawecki**
Co-Owner and Entrepreneur, Gosia's Pierogies
gosiaspierogies.com

**Maria Solovey**
Owner and Designer, Maria Solovey Collection
mariasoloveycollection.com

**Melody Stein**
Co-owner, Mozzeria
mozzeria.com

**Rosetta Stevenson**
Chef and Owner, Zetta Marie's Patisserie
zettamarie.com

**Gina Swanson**
Swanson's Holistic Hands
ginaswanson.com

**Maureen Sydnor**
Owner, Certified Ai Chi and Aqua Kriya Yoga
Aqua Bliss, LLC
aqua-bliss.com

**Jennifer Tandoc**
Artist, Jennifer Tandoc Art
etsy.com/shop/j9artshop

**Melinni "Mel" Taylor**
Owner/Community Partner Work Incentives Counselor,
Deaf Future Works, LLC
deaffutureworks.com

**Dr. Angela K. Trahan**
Advocate & CEO, Deaf Global Solutions
deafglobalsolutions.com

**Anna Virnig**
Co-founder, owner and operations manager
Rawland Cycles, LLC
rawlandcycles.com

**Elise "Lisi" Whitworth**
CEO, Eventida
eventida.com

**Wendy Wiatrowski**
Business owner, Savvy Assistants, LLC
savvyassistants.com

**Dorothy Wilkins**
Certified Yoga Teacher and Certified Life Coach
Deaf Roots and Wings
deafrootsandwings.com

**Melissa Elmira Yingst**
News Anchor and Activist, D-PAN.TV
dpan.tv

**Shiran Zhavian**
Lab Technologist
linkedin.com/in/shiranzhavian

**Heidi Zimmer**
Seven Summits - Heidi Zimmer
heidizimmer.com

**LaRonda Zupp**
Master Retreat & Life Coach
Turtle Heart Coaching & Retreats
turtleheartretreats.com

# Image Descriptions

Front cover: Sixteen black-and-white pictures of diverse smiling women holding various poses cover the outer edges, surrounding a black box. A turquoise starburst is shown in the black box under the title, "The Light of Deaf Women." Under the title is "Inspirational Stories from Visionaries, Artists, Founders & Entrepreneurs," and on the very bottom is "Sofia Seitchik."

Page 6: Iris, a Latina woman with dark hair in a ponytail and glasses, is smiling slightly at the camera and sitting on the floor with her left hand supporting her while her right elbow rests on her right knee as she holds a pair of paintbrushes in her right hand. She is wearing a white top and white pants.

Page 9: Irma, a white woman with shoulder-length dark wavy hair, is standing and smiling at the camera. She is wearing a white tank top with a long white skirt and dark-colored shoes.

Page 10: Page 11: Ally (wearing glasses) and Brittany, two white women with very long, dark hair, are standing side by side holding their pregnant bellies while smiling at the camera. Both are wearing white tops, white pants and Converse shoes.

Page 13: Michelle B., a Black woman with thick dark hair on the top of her head and closely-shaved sides, is standing and smiling at the camera with her hands folded in front of her. She is wearing a white collared shirt with white pants and a necklace with a very large pendant.

Page 14: CyEra, a Black woman with curly short dark hair, has a neutral expression as she looks off-camera towards her right while holding makeup brushes in her hands with her right hand slightly raised and brush near her face. She is wearing a white tank top with a hemp necklace.

Page 17: Keri, a white woman with long wavy light-colored hair, is smiling at the camera while holding a picture of the Mona Lisa in front of her. She is wearing a lacy white top with short sleeves, revealing a tribal tattoo on her left upper arm.

Page 18: Jade, a Black woman with light-colored shoulder-length hair, is smiling widely at the camera while holding a Director's clapboard (slightly blurred) in front of her. She is wearing a white tunic with dark-colored embroidery in the front of the shirt, along the edges of the collar and sleeves.

Page 21: Patty, a white woman with dark hair and light highlights, is slightly smiling at the camera while holding up a white cupcake with white frosting with her right hand. She is wearing a white off-the-shoulder top with straps.

Page 22: Full-length side view of Clare, a white woman with long semi-dark hair, with her left hand on her hip while holding a camera with her right hand and smiling slightly at the camera. She is wearing a long-sleeved white shirt and white pants while barefoot.

Page 25: Maleni, a light-skinned Indian woman with long, dark hair, is smiling slightly at the camera with her arms crossed in front of her. She is wearing a white, buttoned-up shirt with rolled-up sleeves and beaded bracelets on her left wrist.

Page 26: Patricia, a white woman with light-colored hair, is smiling at the camera while standing behind a small podium with a basket on top filled with glass bottles of different sizes and shapes. She is wearing a flowing white top and holding a glass bottle spray with her left hand.

Page 29: Julie D., a white woman with long semi-dark hair, is looking solemnly at the camera while sitting with her back against a wall. She is wearing a white top with various printed and handmade signs next to her: (printed) "Abortion: Safe, Legal & Accessible," (handwritten and hidden behind printed sign) "Abort…, Man….," "Apply!"

Page 30: Jules, a white woman with long semi-dark hair, is smiling slightly at the camera with both hands held up in front of her, framing her face; the hands are slightly blurred. She is wearing a white tee.

Page 33: Julia, a white woman with long dark hair, is smiling at the camera with both hands pressed together in front of her ("Namaste"). She is wearing a white top with long flowing sleeves and large abstract earrings.

Page 34: Brenna, a white woman with very long hair, is smiling at the camera while wearing a white tank top and a dark-colored hat with images and writing on it.

Page 37: Kelly, a white woman with short semi-dark hair with light highlights and glasses, is smiling widely at the camera while sitting on a folding chair with her legs crossed as she leans on her right knee, holding a Canon camera with her right hand crossed in front of her and a miniature painting with paintbrushes in her left hand resting on her knee. She is wearing all white and there is a painting of a dog leaning on the wall behind her.

Page 38: A group of 6 diverse women wearing white clothes are cuddled together smiling/laughing at the camera.

Page 41: Crystal, an Asian woman with long dark wavy hair, is sitting on the floor, smiling at the camera slightly with her right hand resting on the floor and her head slightly tilted. She is wearing a white tee and white pants.

Page 42: Jasmine, an olive-skinned Puerto Rican woman with long dark hair, is smiling widely at the camera with her hands cupping her beaded necklace pendant in front of her. She is wearing a white tank top and white pants.

Page 45: Karen F., a white woman with short light hair, is smiling at the camera, sitting with crossed legs holding a potted plant in front of her. She is wearing a ¾-sleeve top with light-colored pants and white socks.

Page 46: Alli, a white woman with very short hair, is smiling at the camera wearing a white top with a dark-colored necklace.

Page 49: Suzette, a olive-skinned Latina woman, is sitting on the floor with her right hand supporting her body and smiling at the camera while she holds a sign in front of her with her left hand which has the following text: "It isn't what we say or think that defines us but what we DO. ~Jane Austen." She is wearing a long-sleeve collared button-up shirt and white pants.

Page 50: A full-length side view of Arlene, a light-skinned Puerto Rican woman with medium-length dark hair, who is smiling at the camera with her hands on her hips. She is wearing a white tee and white pants with dark-colored heels.

Page 53: Haydee, a Cuban woman with dark short curly hair held back by a cloth headband and glasses, is smiling at the camera while wearing a backpack, holding it with her left hand and in her right hand, holding a miniature globe. She is wearing a ¾-sleeved white top.

Page 54: Claudia, a Black woman with closely cropped hair, is sitting on a chair crossed-legged with her chin resting on her left hand as she smiles at the camera. She is wearing a white dress with a white and see-through gingham pattern.

Page 57: Melissa G., a white woman with long light-colored hair, is smiling at the camera while sitting on the floor with her hands resting on her crossed legs. She is wearing a white buttoned-up shirt and white pants with a dark-colored pillow leaning against the wall behind her.

Page 58: Smitha, an Indian woman with long dark hair, is smiling widely at the camera with her elbows close to her body and arms up. She is wearing a mostly light-colored sari that has some dark coloring on her right shoulder and at the sari edges.

Page 61: Laural, a white woman with shoulder-length wavy dark hair, is smiling at the camera while in her left arm she is holding a print of the sign BOSTON with the word above it and a measuring instrument in her right hand. She is wearing a lacy white tee with white pants.

Page 62: (l to r) Lauren (white woman), Kavita (Indian woman), and Lisa (white woman) are cuddled together, smiling/laughing at the camera while Lauren and Lisa are holding each other's arms. All are wearing white clothes.

Page 65: Peggy, a white woman with short semi-dark hair, is leaning towards the camera with her left side and smiling while she signs TEACH.

Page 66: Elise H., a white woman with shoulder-length dark hair, is smiling at the camera with her arms folded in front of her. She is wearing a long-sleeved white top with light-colored drapes behind her and a patterned shirt hanging on a hook slightly behind her.

Page 69: Tawny, a white woman with semi-dark shoulder-length hair and glasses, is smiling at the camera. She is wearing a white top with a white jacket, a necklace of large pearls and small beads, and pearl earrings.

Page 70: Monique, a Korean woman with short white hair that has dark undertones, is gazing downwards with pursed lips and one arm stretched as if taking a selfie. She is wearing a white top with a dark-colored scarf wrapped around her neck.

Page 73: Sabrina, a white woman with long hair dark at the top and light at the ends, is standing away from the camera with her head turned towards it and smiling. She is wearing heels and a light-colored off-the-shoulder dress with straps that is fitted at the top, flowing from waist down.

Page 74: Vicki, a white woman with short gray hair and glasses, is smiling at the camera while holding up the end of her colored scarf with her right hand. She is wearing a long-sleeved lacy top along with a metallic bracelet on her right arm.

Page 77: Lynn, a white woman with glasses and very short curly dark hair, is smiling slightly at the camera while holding her tie in front of her with both hands as if adjusting it.

Page 78: A group of 5 diverse women wearing white clothes are cuddled together smiling at the camera.

Page 81: Rochella, a white woman with very long semi-dark hair in a ponytail hanging down her left side, is laughing as she holds a chicken in her arms with a table to her right, on top of which has a wire basket of fresh eggs, vitamin bottles, and tubes of products. She is wearing a short white dress with short sleeves.

Page 82: Leah, a Latina/white woman with long dark hair, is standing and smiling at the camera with her hands in front of her and her right foot in front of her left. She is wearing a sleeveless white business dress and dark peep-toe heels.

Page 85: Mara, a Filipina woman with dark hair piled up on top of her head in a bun, is smiling at the camera with her hands partially in the pockets of her buttoned-up shirt styled dress. She is wearing light-colored ankle-cuff heels with a wooden pallet standing up on its side directly behind her.

Page 86: (l to r) Katherine, a white woman with a light-colored hair in a pixie cut, and Michelle, a white woman with long semi-dark wavy hair, are both wearing sunglasses and slightly smiling at the camera. Both are wearing white tops and popping their collars while wearing watches and bracelets.

Page 89: Rosemary, a white woman with long dark hair, is smiling slightly at the camera with her arms crossed and a table in front of her with a LSU cake, a cake decorated with roses and the word "love," a platter on a stand with several cupcakes on it, and flower cookies laid out in front of everything. She is wearing a white chef's jacket with black trim at the sides, neckline, and cuffs.

Page 90: Sheena, a black woman with long dark dreadlocks with light ends, is smiling at the camera slightly with her arms outstretched; her left arm is tattooed. She is wearing a white hat with a white tee and a necklace.

Page 93: Melissa M., a white woman with shoulder-length light-colored hair, is standing and slightly smiling at the camera with her left hand on her hip and right arm resting by her side. She is wearing a white sleeveless top and white pants with dark-colored booties.

Page 94: Marlee, a white woman with long light-colored hair, is smiling at the camera while holding up her Oscar trophy. She is wearing a white long-sleeved blouse and a large watch on her left wrist.

Page 97: Lori, a white woman with shoulder-length light-colored hair, is smiling at the camera while holding a wrapped sage smudge stick in her left hand which is below a feather with a decorated handle held horizontally in her left hand. She is wearing a white

buttoned-up shirt.

Page 98: (l to r) Candace, a white woman with short curly hair and folded arms, and Sharon, a white woman with a very short hair and her right hand clasping her left wrist, are both smiling at the camera angled slightly upwards. They are wearing long-sleeved white tops.

Page 101: Ann, a white woman with very short white short hair and glasses, is smiling at the camera while holding a SOLD sign. She is wearing a white top with a white jean jacket.

Page 102: Malene, a white woman with short dark hair and glasses, is smiling slightly while looking away from the camera towards the left of the picture. She is wearing a white blazer and necklace with black string with the letters L, O, V, E strung on it.

Page 105: Rebecca, a white woman with long dark hair, is smiling at the camera while hold a pair of scissors in each hand. She is wearing a V-neck white top with strings hanging down from the neckline.

Page 106: Sarah, a white woman with short dark hair and glasses, is smiling at the camera while holding her white cane with a black handle in her right hand close to her body while her left hand lightly rests on her hip. She is wearing a white tee with a white buttoned-up collared shirt and white pants with a dark-colored belt.

Page 109: Dawnena, a Native American woman with dark hair in two long braids on either side of her and a feather hanging down from her head, is smiles slightly at the camera with her hands clasped in front of her. She is wearing a traditional beaded light-colored leather Native American top.

Page 110: Irina, an olive-skinned woman with long wavy dark hair and glasses, is smiling at the camera and signing JOY. She is wearing a white button-up shirt and has a pair of beaded cuffs on her wrists.

Page 113: Side view of Gina, a white woman with dark hair in a ponytail, smiling at the camera with a cloth bag over her left arm as she holds it with her left hand and her right hand on the handles. She is wearing a ¾-sleeve white top with white pants.

Page 114: (l to r) Leah (Latina/white woman), Claudia (Black woman), and Michelle (Black woman), all are cuddled together, smiling at the camera and wearing white clothes. Leah and Michelle are holding each other's arms.

Page 117: Joette, a white woman with long gray-white hair, is smiling at the camera with her left hand on her hip and her right hand covering her stomach. She is wearing a white top with a white buttoned-up long-sleeve shirt left open and white pants.

Page 118: Karen P., a white woman with shoulder-length semi-dark hair, is smiling slightly at the camera while sitting on the floor with her right leg crossed over on top of her left leg. She is wearing a white long-sleeve top and flowy white pants.

Page 121: Rajarajeshwari, a white woman with long dark hair, is sitting crossed-legged yoga-style and smiling at the camera while holding a bunch of lei flowers in front of her. She is wearing a white tank top with a lei around her neck and white pants as bunches of lei flowers are in mid-air on either side of her.

Page 122: Rez, an Eritrean-American woman with dark hair and shoulder-length dreadlocks, is looking at the camera solemnly as she adjusts her white tie paired with a white collared button-up shirt; sleeves are rolled up.

Page 125: Jesica, a Latina woman with shoulder-length dark hair held back with a bandana, is smiling at the camera while flexing her left arm on which 6 handmade soaps are piled on. She is wearing a lacy white top,

several bracelets on her left wrist, and large shell circle earrings.

Page 126: Jackie, a white woman with short dark hair, is smiling slightly at the camera while wearing a white top and multiple necklaces.

Page 129: Nancy, a white woman with long semi-dark long hair, is smiling at the camera while leaning on a small table with her left elbow and left hand holding a paintbrush. Her legs are crossed and her right hand rests on her left thigh. On the small table is a painting she did with fingerspelled letters L, O, V, E on an easel with a tube of paint and more paintbrushes in front of it. She is wearing a tee with her artwork on it and light-colored pants.

Page 130: Nicki, a white woman with long dark hair, is smiling at the camera and with outstretched arms holding dark-colored shiny theatre masks (left one has a frown while right one has a smile). She is wearing a light-colored top.

Page 133: Terrylene, a white woman with short dark hair, is smiling slightly off camera with her arms slightly outstretched in front of her. She is wearing a white ¾-sleeve half-buttoned blouse made of thin material.

Page 134: Sofia, an olive-skinned woman with long dark wavy hair, is smiling slightly at the camera while her hands are pressed together in front of her ("Namaste"). She is wearing a white top with a necklace that has large beads.

Page 137: Virginia, an Asian woman with long dark hair, is smiling slightly at the camera while holding a potted plant with her left hand. She is wearing a light-colored floppy felt hat, a patterned scarf, a long necklace, and a bracelet on her left wrist.

Page 138: Mary, a white woman with short blonde hair, is smiling at the camera while sitting on the floor holding a cup of water in her right hand and paintbrushes in her left hand. She is wearing a white tee, white pants and shiny, metallic shoes. Behind her is a wooden pallet standing on its end with wooden paint board leaning against the pallet and a painting of a lotus flower with "Dream" above it hanging on the pallet.

Page 141: Julie S., a white woman with short light hair, is smiling and looking towards the right of the picture. She is wearing a white off-the-shoulder dress with dark embroidery of miniature flowers and large roses along the top part of the dress along with a necklace.

Page 142: Marilyn, a white woman with short blonde hair, is smiling at the camera with her right fist on her hip and her left hand held up in front of her. She is wearing a white ¾-sleeve lacy top.

Page 145: Storm, a Black woman with very long curly dark hair, is smiling at the camera while holding a Director's clapboard in front of her. She is wearing a light-colored collared button-up shirt.

Page 146: Terry, a white woman with short light-colored hair and glasses, is smiling at the camera while holding a large frying pan placed on a stand with pierogies in it and in her right hand, a pair of metal tongs. She is wearing a white tee with the words "Gosia's Pierogies" and image of a chef on her upper left side.

Page 149: A group of 4 diverse women wearing white clothes are cuddled together all smiling/laughing; (l-r) 1st woman is looking down, 2nd woman is looking at the camera, 3rd woman is looking upwards, and 4th woman is looking at 3rd woman.

Page 150: Maria, a Ukrainian woman with long dyed blonde hair, is smiling at the camera along with a white girl, Princess Lola, standing to Maria's right. Both are wearing white dresses; Maria has a white coat over her dress and she is holding a square box filled with roses standing on their stems inside.

Page 153: Melody, an Asian woman with dark hair tied back, is smiling at the camera with her hands on her hips (photo is taken from chest up). She is wearing a white v-neck long-sleeve shirt.

Page 154: Page 165: Rosetta, a Black woman with dark dreadlocks tied back, is smiling at the camera while holding a ring cake in each hand (left one is dark with white frosting and right one is light with dark/light coloring on top). She is wearing a light-colored tee which has the words "Zetta Marie's Patisserie" written on it with an image of a cake in the middle.

Page 157: Gina S., a white woman with long light-colored hair wearing glasses, is smiling slightly at the camera and wearing white angel wings on her back while holding three small items in front of her: a crystal rock, an oracle card tarot box, and a white angel statue. She is wearing a long-sleeve white top with white pants.

Page 158: Maureen, a white woman with short light-colored hair, is smiling slightly at the camera while holding large meditation balls in both hands. She is wearing a long white dress with fringes at the bottom hem, a chunky necklace, and an anklet toe ring made of white beads and pearls.

Page 161: Jennifer, an olive-skinned woman with long dark hair, is smiling at the camera while sitting on the floor and holding a poster-sized black and white ink drawing with her right hand. She is wearing a white top, white pants, and black sandals.

Page 162: Melinni, a white woman with very short dark hair and glasses, is smiling at the camera while with holding up an iPhone in her left hand with the calculator app open and her right fist on her hip. She is wearing a white lacy sleeveless top.

Page 165: Angela, a white woman with shoulder-length semi-dark hair wearing glasses, is looking solemnly at the camera while signing ADVOCATE. She is wearing a white tee with a bracelet on her left wrist.

Page 166: Anna, a white woman with short dark hair, is smiling slightly at the camera while holding the triangular part of a bicycle frame over her right shoulder. She is wearing a long-sleeved white top with a hood covering part of her head.

Page 169: Elise W., a white woman with very long light-colored hair, is smiling at the camera with her hands on her hips. She is wearing a white tank top with a necklace with a butterfly pendant.

Pahe 170: Wendy, a white woman with light-colored shoulder-length hair and glasses, is sitting with her legs in front of her and smiling at the camera while she has an open clipboard in front of her with her right hand holding a pen, ready to write; her left hand is resting on her left knee. She is barefoot and wearing a white tank top, white pants, and a long necklace.

Page 173: Dorothy, a white woman with very short white hair and glasses, is smiling at the camera with her hands pressed together in front of her chest ("Namaste"). She is wearing a white tee with a mala necklace and bracelet of stone beads on her right wrist.

Page 174: Melissa Y., a Mexicana woman with long semi-dark hair, is slightly smiling at the camera while holding her phone pointed towards her in front of her as she leans over a dark-colored chair. She is wearing a white top with a white long-sleeve jacket.

Page 177: Shiran, an Israeli woman with long dark hair, is standing and smiling at the camera with her hands inside the pockets of a long white lab coat. In addition to the coat, she is wearing a white collared button-up shirt, white pants, and dark-colored low heels.

Page 178: Heidi, a white woman with short light-colored hair, is smiling at the camera while wearing white clothes, a hiking backpack, hiking boots and resting her right arm on a pair of hiking poles.

Page 181: LaRonda, a white woman with long semi-dark colored hair, is smiling slightly and looking towards the right of the picture as she holds her arms up. She is wear a white top with a flowing robe over it.

Page 182: (l to r) Irina and Sofia, both olive-skinned women with long dark wavy hair, are standing with one hand on their hips, mirror opposites of each other, and smiling at the camera. They are wearing white tops and pants; Irina has beaded cuffs on both wrists while Sofia has wearing a necklace with large beads and a white watch.

Back cover: Sofia, an olive-skinned woman with long dark wavy hair, is smiling at the camera. She is wearing a white top with a necklace that has large beads.